ENGLISH LANGUAGE TODAY

English Language Today

E. LORING and A. H. LAWLEY

HUTCHINSON EDUCATIONAL

HUTCHINSON EDUCATIONAL LTD
3 Fitzroy Square, London W1

London Melbourne Sydney Auckland
Wellington Johannesburg Cape Town
and agencies throughout the world

First published 1972
Reprinted, with answers, 1974

Printed in Great Britain by The Anchor Press Ltd,
and bound by Wm. Brendon & Son Ltd,
both of Tiptree, Essex

ISBN 0 09 120681 2

CONTENTS

PREFACE

The purpose of this book is twofold: first, to extend students' ability to understand what they read and to write interesting, effective English; second, to help candidates to pass in English Language at Ordinary level or to prepare themselves for a C.S.E. Examination in English. The book includes fourteen test papers containing the sorts of questions now commonly used. Teachers have urged the Boards to avoid trivial points of grammar and isolated tests of vocabulary and punctuation; instead they have demanded more varied and creative exercises in writing, and comprehension questions based on more interesting extracts.

In constructing the tests in this book we have tried to do more than prepare candidates for an examination. We have chosen extracts which can be read for pleasure as though the book were a straightforward anthology, and which will also serve as models for the pupils' own writing. Further, we have tried to encourage creative writing by the topics we have set.

Since most examining boards are planning to allot about 35 per cent of the marks to objective tests, this book contains plenty of examples of this form of comprehension test. Besides leading to fairer marking, they also have the important virtue that they train students more widely—to understand the meanings of individual words, to relate them to their context, to see the relevance of metaphors or similes or examples, to follow the ideas of a writer, to read between the lines and respond to a writer's emotion or intention, to recognise irony, and to make deductions from what is merely implied as well as what is openly stated.

E.L.
A.H.L.

CHAPTER ONE

Writing an Essay

1 *Choosing the Subject*

Where you are given a choice of subjects, choose the one which you know most about. In this way you will be more likely to interest the reader; all readers, including examiners, prefer to be interested rather than bored. Should you have any relevant personal experiences about which you can write with freshness and conviction, choose a title which enables you to use them. The more the subject interests you, the more likely you are to include convincing detail. If the topic is your home or family, using authentic incidents may entertain the reader and show your power of observation.

If you are asked to write on a factual subject such as 'The Effects of Crop-spraying on Wild Flowers', it is useless to attempt this unless you have recently read a book about the subject or seen a good television programme on it. Similarly, it would be foolish to choose the subject 'Television Serials' if you did not watch them, or 'Photography' or 'Swimming' if neither of these pursuits interests you.

To sum up then, choose as your topic the one that you are most interested in or are most knowledgeable about. Then you will write most convincingly about it.

2 *Relevance*

Irrelevance is a serious fault. This may result from careless reading or interpretation of the title. Candidates in examinations lose marks unnecessarily by writing about 'Comprehensive Schools' when the subject is 'Co-educational Schools', or about their favourite 'country' when asked to describe their favourite 'county'.

Be careful about plurals; if asked to write on 'The Pleasures of Winter', you ought not to concentrate on *one* pleasure. Watch for the keyword in a title; if the subject is 'The Fascination of Railways', the word 'fascination' must be kept in mind and any other aspects of railways excluded.

Irrelevance can creep in during the writing of an essay. A candidate may begin by writing quite closely on the subject but drift off it and introduce material which has no direct bearing on the title. It is useful to remind yourself from time to time of the exact wording. If it is 'The Pleasures of Life in a Large Town', do not write about the disadvantages of life in a large town or the pleasures of life in a small town. If your topic is 'A Lucky Escape', you need to start your story at the point where the danger begins to develop. You should tell the early part of the story very briefly, devoting most space to the danger and to your escape.

3 Planning the Essay

Be prepared to spend some time assembling material for your essay before you start writing. Make rough notes of ideas, putting them in order. Do not begin the essay until you have made this outline. It is helpful to the examiner if you cross through all this preparatory work when you have finished with it. An essay of about 450 words (the usual length for an 'O'-level essay) will normally contain four to six paragraphs. Each of these should deal with one aspect of the subject or one stage in the narrative.

4 The First Paragraph

You want to arouse the interest of your reader straight away, so it is worth while spending time on giving your essay a good beginning, like the boy who wrote:

> The pleasures of being one of a large family may well be more apparent to an only child than to one who is the youngest of a family of nine.

A bad mistake is to assume too little knowledge in your reader. Beginning an essay with such obvious remarks as 'Television is an electrical instrument which can show us a picture', or 'The moon is a very long way from the earth', or

'The amount of traffic in our towns is continually increasing'
will antagonise your reader. He knows such elementary things.
You should assume that he is informed and intelligent and try
to establish friendly relations with him as quickly as possible.

Begin with something obviously important and relevant.
Avoid the temptation to start with a long irrelevant history
lesson; if you are writing about Modern Industry, you do not
need to begin with an account of the Industrial Revolution or
the invention of the wheel.

5   *Styles of Writing*

Some titles invite you to tell a story, but it is important not to
do so unless the title justifies it. If you are asked to write on
'The Dangers of Deep-Sea Diving', you would be penalised if
you merely wrote an account of one dangerous incident. But if
the title is 'A Lucky Escape' or if you are given the first sentence
of a story and invited to continue it, then obviously narrative
is expected.

Some topics seem to invite a chatty style of writing, but you
must remember that in an examination the main thing is to
convince your reader that you can write correctly and formally.
It is better, therefore, to avoid colloquial words and phrases
which, while acceptable in conversation, are not fitting in an
essay. Avoid abbreviations such as 'I'll', 'can't' and 'isn't' and
overworked words such as 'nice', 'terrible' and 'awfully'.

6   *Paragraph Connection*

While it is important to confine each paragraph to one topic it is
also important to link your paragraphs together so that your
essay reads as a continuous piece of writing. In each paragraph
your first sentence may well be a topic sentence indicating the
subject of that paragraph; but it can also show its connection
with the previous paragraph by the inclusion of some word or
phrase such as 'nevertheless', 'however', 'moreover', or 'in
addition'. For instance, in switching from the disadvantages of
being an only child to the advantages, you could use bridging
sentences:

e.g. There are, however, many advantages in being an

only child. Although I was nervous as a child, I was always quite at ease with my grandfather.

The introduction of a new topic at the end of a paragraph can act as a link with the next. A paragraph which had dealt with the advantages of living in the country might end with a sentence like this:

There is, however, another consideration to bear in mind: will the country seem equally attractive when snow-drifts have isolated your cottage?

This prepares your reader for your next paragraph—on the disadvantages.

7 *The Last Paragraph*

Just as the first paragraph gives a reader his first impression of the quality of your work, so the last is the one which is most in his mind when he is considering what mark to give you. It is important, therefore, to take particular care to give an effective ending to your essay, one which is not just a dull repetition or summary of what you have already said, but a climax. Sometimes it is possible to make some reference in your last sentence to the title of the essay, as does J. B. Priestley when, in the last sentence of his essay 'Detective Stories in Bed', he refers to both parts of the title:

. . . and what a delight it is to stretch legs that have begun to ache a little, turn on the right side, and then once more to find the eccentric private detective moodily playing his violin or tending his orchids, or discover again the grumpy inspector doodling in his office, and know that a still more astonishing puzzle is on its way to him and to me!

8 *Revision*

In planning the writing of your essay you must leave sufficient time for a thorough revision of what you have written. We all make careless mistakes when writing quickly and need to re-read carefully and critically to remove them. Errors of spelling, grammar, punctuation and omission mean loss of marks if not put right before the work is handed in. It is a great mistake to be writing until the very end and you should leave yourself about five minutes for this final re-reading and improving.

TEST 1

A   Write a composition of about 450 words on one of the following subjects:

   1 Careers I should not like to follow
   2 Two young people in the news whom I admire
   3 A frightening experience—real or imaginary
   4 The value of school journeys abroad
   5 Our family's first car
   6 How my town or village could be made a more attractive place to live in
   7 Some differences between parents and grandparents
   8 Write a story or a description or an essay suggested by the picture facing page 96

B 1 Write a letter to a television company expressing approval or disapproval of one of its regular programmes
   2 Three persons of your age have advertised for a fourth to join them on a car tour through France and Spain. Write expressing interest and giving such information about yourself as seems relevant
   3 You are secretary of a school society which wishes to visit a house of historic interest. Write a letter to the owner asking permission to do so and giving him all relevant information
   4 What can be said for and against one of the following:
      (a) submerging hill farms to make a reservoir
      (b) subsidising a branch railway line
      (c) giving loans instead of grants to students?
   5 Write a letter to the Head of your school, on behalf of the pupils of your village, in which you complain about the inadequacies of the bus service to and from school and ask the Head to take whatever action he thinks fit

6 Imagine that you are a member of a committee set up to advise the Prime Minister on whether this country should spend any considerable amount of money on research connected with Space Travel. Your committee has discussed a number of points, including those listed below. Write a report advising the Prime Minister on a course of action, indicating the main arguments in favour of your decision.

[Very expensive. Even if we could reach a planet, the journey would take very long time. Western Europe or British Commonwealth could combine to compete with Russia and U.S.A. Nations leading in space race may have military advantage. Space research might lead indirectly to important scientific discoveries. Money wasted on space travel might have been used to prevent world starvation. A country ignoring space research might find best scientists emigrating. Ought we to attach less importance to prestige? Would stimulate industry, e.g. electronics. Dangers to astronauts. Satellites to help communications (Telstar), weather forecasting, and navigation, Harmless outlet for man's adventurous and combative instincts. Effective advertisement for our other products in world markets.]

Section II SUMMARY AND COMPREHENSION

1 Read the following review of Sir Christopher Andrewes's book, *The Common Cold*. Write four paragraphs

(a) in 100 words explaining why it is both important and difficult to prevent the common cold
(b) in 40 words explaining how it was proved that a cold is due to a virus
(c) in 80 words explaining what progress has been made at Salisbury in research into the common cold
(d) in 30 words explaining how you could have deduced from its context that *serendipity* means 'the faculty of making happy and unexpected discoveries by accident'

Laymen suspect that because colds are self-limiting, short, non-fatal infections doctors do not take them very seriously.

Nobody will think this after reading Sir Christopher
Andrewes's book.

An American survey has shown that each year every em-   5
ployed person loses three to four working days from colds and
allied complaints, and every school child loses five to six days
of schooling. Colds waste more time than strikes. The
conquest of the common cold is therefore a thoroughly
worthwhile ambition.   10

Until 1961 Sir Christopher Andrewes was in charge of the
Medical Research Council's Common Cold Research Unit at
Salisbury, and he writes as one of the world's experts when he
describes the patience, the frustrations, the ingenuity and
occasional flashes of true scientific genius which have   15
characterised the careers of the workers who have set out to
tackle what has turned out to be a real brute of a problem.

The great killing infections like syphilis or poliomyelitis
are each caused by one specific micro-organism, or, at worst,
a small group of closely related parasites.... By contrast it has   20
slowly become apparent that the common cold is not a disease
but a large group of similar diseases, caused, possibly, by anything between fifty and one hundred different organisms.

Much of Sir Christopher's book is taken up by an account
of the struggle to identify the germs which do cause colds.   25
At first it was thought that bacteria were responsible because
certain bacteria are commonly found in the noses and throats
of cold victims. The first evidence that a virus might be concerned was obtained in 1914 when Dr W. Kruse of the
Hygienic Institute of the University of Leipzig took some of   30
the discharge from the nose of an assistant with a cold in the
head, diluted the discharge in saline, and then passed it
through a filter with pores too small to permit the passage of
bacteria. Drops of the filtrate were put into the noses of
twelve other members of the staff and four of them developed   35
colds within a day or so.

Since that time thousands of volunteers have subjected
themselves to similar experimental infections, and for nearly
twenty years most of such work has been done at Salisbury
where the guinea pigs are rewarded by a ten-day holiday, all   40
found. . . . This 'clumsy, expensive and unreliable' use of
human volunteers was necessary because for a long time

chimpanzees were the only other animals known to be susceptible to infection by common cold germs, and chimpanzees were far too expensive and unruly for routine use. 45

Growing cold viruses in the laboratory also proved difficult until one of the men involved demonstrated his possession of that most precious scientific faculty—*serendipity*.

Cold viruses were being grown with only moderate success in laboratory cultures of lung tissue from human embryos. 50 The lung tissue cultures were kept alive by a salt solution containing added vitamins and a number of other ingredients. One day at Salisbury Dr David Tyrrell found that his salt solution was faulty, and in order to keep his tissue cultures 55 going he hastily borrowed a supply from another laboratory. When the imported solution was added to tissue cultures infected with cold viruses, the lung tissue cells began to degenerate in a manner typical of tissues parasitised by active viral particles. 60

Dr Tyrrell soon discovered that the borrowed fluid provided a more acid medium in his culture tubes than that produced by the native Salisbury brew. The nose provides a slightly acid environment, and Dr Tyrrell realised that a degree of acidity was just what nose-inhabiting viruses 65 needed in order to thrive outside the body. Thus a happy accident enabled a perspicacious scientist to modify the cold virus culture technique, and thenceforward the whole exercise proved far easier and more profitable.

Much of common cold folklore is demolished. Draughts, 70 chilling and wet feet do not bring colds on, says Sir Christopher, and clean, healthy living with lots of fresh air, plenty of exercise, good, plain food and a cold bath every morning may be good for the soul and the waistline, but does nothing to keep cold viruses at bay. 75

Colds are not very infectious (which will surprise most of us), so there is really no excuse for staying away from work when you have one. All the remedies so far invented have one thing in common—they are useless. In temperate countries, colds are commoner during the winter, but what 80 the 'winter factor' is which brings them on remains unknown. Most of us harbour cold viruses in our noses throughout

the year, and many colds are probably not 'caught' at all, but
start because somehow the resident viruses become activated
from time to time.   85

To write a book about colds at this stage, says Sir Christopher, is rather like writing a review of a play in the middle of
the first act. Since he wrote those words, workers at Salisbury
have announced the production of the first cold vaccine which
will protect against infection by one particular cold virus.   90
Unfortunately there are very many cold viruses, and complete
immunity from colds by vaccination would require the ad-
ministration of a separate vaccine for every virus in the book.

2 Read the following passage (which for your convenience
  has been divided into three sections) and answer the
  questions which follow it.

A

A medical examination at school had revealed the fact that
I was short-sighted. The doctor took me solemnly between
his knees, looked into my face, and said, 'If you don't get
some glasses, you'll be blind by the time you are fifteen, and
I shall tell your parents so.'   5

I was rather proud of this distinction. Fifteen! That was
so far ahead that it meant nothing to me, except a sort of
twilight at the end of life. My parents thought otherwise, and
one Saturday afternoon I was taken, via a steep road called
Pig Hill, to a chemist's shop on Lavender Hill, Clapham,   10
opposite the first theatre I was ever to enter, 'The Shakespeare'. Behind the shop was a room where my eyes were
tested in the rough and ready way customary in those days.
The chemist hung an open framework that felt like the
Forth Bridge around my ears and on my nose. Lenses were   15
slotted into this, and twisted about, while I was instructed to
read the card of letters beginning with a large 'E'.

I still remember the astonishment with which I saw the
smaller letters change from a dark blur into separate items of
the alphabet. I thought about it all the following week, and   20
found that by screwing up my eyes when I was out of doors
I could get some faint approximation of that clarity, for a
few seconds at a time.

This made me surmise that the universe which hitherto
I had seen as a vague mass of colour and blurred shapes   25
might in actuality be much more concise and defined. I was
therefore half-prepared for the surprise which shook me a
week later when, on the Saturday evening, we went again
to the shop on Lavender Hill, and the chemist produced the
bespoken pair of steel-rimmed spectacles through which I was   30
invited to read the card. I read it, from top to bottom! I
turned, and looked in triumph at Mother, but what I saw
was Mother intensified. I saw the pupils of her eyes, the tiny
feathers in her boa necklet; I saw the hairs in Father's
moustache, and on the back of his hand. Jack's cap might   35
have been made of metal, so hard and clear did it shine on his
close-cropped head, above his bony face and huge nose.
I saw *his* eyes too, round, inquiring, fierce with a hunger of
observation. He was studying me with a gimlet sharpness
such as I had never before been able to perceive.   40

B

Then we walked out of the shop, and I stepped on to the
pavement, which came up and hit me, so that I had to grasp
the nearest support—Father's coat. 'Take care, now take care!'
he said indulgently (though he disapproved of all these conces-
sions to physical weakness). 'And mind you don't break them!'   5
I walked, still with some uncertainty, carefully placing my
feet and feeling their impact on the pavement whose surface
I could see sparkling like quartz in the lamplight. The lamplight! I looked in wonder at the diminishing crystals of gas-
flame strung down the hill. Clapham was hung with necklaces   10
of light, and the horses pulling the glittering omnibuses
struck the granite road with hooves of iron and ebony. I
could see the skeletons inside the flesh and blood of the
Saturday-night shoppers. The garments they wore were
made of separate threads. In this new world, sound as well   15
as sight was changed. It took on hardness and definition,
forcing itself upon my hearing, so that I was besieged
simultaneously through the eye and through the ear.
How willingly I surrendered! I went out to meet this
blazing and trumpeting invasion. I trembled with the   20
excitement, and had to cling to Mother's arm to prevent

myself being carried away in the flood as the pavements
rushed at me, and people loomed up with their teeth like
tusks, their lips luscious, their eyes bolting out of their heads,
bearing down on me as they threw out spears of conversation   25
that whizzed loudly past my ears and bewildered my wits.

C

By the time we reached the darker streets near home, my
head ached under the burden of too much seeing. Perhaps the
grease of the fried fish, and the lateness of the hour, had
something to do with the exhaustion that almost destroyed
me as we trailed homeward. The new spectacles clung to   5
my face, eating into the bridge of my nose and behind the
earlobes. I longed to tear them off and throw them away into
the darkness. I tried to linger behind so that at least I might
secrete them in the pocket of my blouse.

But before I could further this purpose, something caught   10
my attention. I realised that, after all, the side-streets were
not quite dark; that the yellow pools round each gas-lamp,
now as clearly defined as golden sovereigns, were aug-
mented, pervaded, suffused by a bluish silver glory. I looked
upward, and saw the sky. And in that sky I saw an almost full   15
moon, floating in space, a solid ball of roughened metal, with
an irregular jagged edge. I could put up my hand and take
it, ponder its weight, feel its cold surface.

I stopped walking, and stared. I turned up my face, throw-
ing back my head to look vertically into the zenith. I saw the   20
stars, and I saw them for the first time, a few only, for most
were obscured by the light of the moon; but those I saw were
clean pin-points of light, diamond-hard, standing not upon
a velvet surface, but floating in space, some near, some far,
in an awe-striking perspective that came as a revelation to   25
my newly-educated eyes.

From Section A

1 Give in a single word or phrase the meaning of: customary
   (l. 13), surmise (l. 24), intensified (l. 33), perceive (l. 40)
2 Explain what the author (Richard Church) meant by: an
   open framework that felt like the Forth Bridge (ll. 14–15),

some faint approximation of that clarity (l. 22), studying me with gimlet sharpness (l. 39)

3 What does he mean by saying that fifteen was 'a sort of twilight at the end of life' (ll. 7–8)?

4 Why was he half-prepared for the surprise he experienced when he put on his new glasses?

5 How does he stress the effect of putting them on?

From Section B

6 Explain the following as used in the passage: indulgently (l. 4), simultaneously (l. 18), this blazing and trumpeting invasion (l. 20)

7 Quote and comment on two words he uses to show his new impressions of (a) the pavements (b) the gas lamps (c) the omnibuses

8 How does he convey the new awareness of people's faces and their conversation?

From Section C

9 Give another word or phrase for the following: exhaustion (l. 4), secrete (l. 9), obscured (l. 22), revelation (l. 25)

10 Comment on the effectiveness of the sentence 'I looked upward and saw the sky' (ll. 14–15)

11 Quote and comment on his description of (a) the moon (b) the stars as he now saw them

12 What part of speech is the word 'further' in l. 10? Write a sentence using it as a different part of speech and name it

From the whole passage

13 The new glasses had advantages but also disadvantages. In two sentences, each of about 20 words, point out what these were

14 How does the writer convey the boy's feelings during this episode?

15 In about a page *either* write the letter that Richard Church's mother might have written to her sister describing these events *or* describe an incident in your own life that has some small similarity to this incident in Church's life, stressing your feelings resulting from the incident

CHAPTER TWO

Creative Writing

Nowadays some of the questions set in examinations give you the chance to write openly about your own experiences. These sometimes stimulate good writing; they allow you to write freely about your private thoughts and feelings.

To write like this you have to conquer your shyness and trust your teacher or examiner to be tactful and read sympathetically what you have written. You need to believe that your reader is open-minded and interested in your reactions. Write in order to share your experiences with him. Set down your ideas in a way that is personal to you but will also interest others. You must write honestly about your adventures, thoughts, ideas, hopes and fears. Be spontaneous, and on your guard against writing what you think is expected; you can only write convincingly if the feelings you lay claim to are genuine.

One of your problems in this sort of writing is how near you should get to the spoken word. Control your first impulse to use too many abbreviations and too many colloquial words, or to imitate too closely the broken rhythms and short sentences of informal speech. Even in modern novels the writing shows a degree of control and shaping that actual speech lacks. Plan your sentences and present your material in a logical order. Writing is always more thoughtful and orderly than speech, and writing down your thoughts often helps you to sort them out. You need to think about what has happened to you in the past, to select the most interesting events that have occurred and to put them in a sensible order before you begin to write. You will need to draw sensitively on your stock of memories and your stock of words to express them.

As an example of creative writing, let us take this description from D. H. Lawrence's *Women in Love* of how Gerald Crick forces the mare he is riding to stand in terror at a level-crossing while a train of coal-trucks goes past:

'The locomotive chuffed slowly between the banks, hidden. The mare did not like it. She began to wince away, as if hurt by the unknown noise. But Gerald pulled her back and held her head to the gate. The sharp blasts of the chuffing engine broke with more and more force on her. The repeated sharp blows of unknown, terrifying noise struck through her till she was rocking with terror. She recoiled like a spring let go. But a glistening half-smiling look came into Gerald's face. He brought her back again, inevitably.'

Lawrence makes us feel the terror of the animal and hear the noise of the engine in the way that the terrified horse hears it. The clever selection of words such as *chuffed* and *sharp blasts*, and of similes and metaphors that compare the noise to blows, or the horse to a recoiling spring, help to make us feel the noise of the engine and the reaction of the horse. As you read, you almost convince yourself that you have heard the train just as the horse heard it. If you keep your eyes and ears open as you move about, and practise thinking of words or phrases to describe exactly what you see and hear, then your own writing can develop some of the qualities of Lawrence's. Sharp observation of life will make you notice more than before; it will also help you to write interesting English by using vivid phrases. Try to look at some familiar scene, like your own street or the view from your classroom window, as though you are seeing it for the first time, and try to find words and sentences to record, in a sort of diary, how you feel. This will give your English vitality and will help it illustrate your perception. You will see things more vividly and feel more intensely about them.

In writing like this, try to avoid stock phrases such as 'in this day and age' that you have read or heard many times; never use a fashionable word when you can think of a simpler one; take the same view of language as the modern poet, Ted Hughes, took in a B.B.C. broadcast—'Make it True, Make it New, Make it You.' Your writing must have energy, must be your own, and be positive and forceful. It must also seem authentic and sincere; others must feel that you really felt what you claimed to feel.

Here are some brief extracts from examples of creative writing produced by pupils of fifteen. One writer gives an interesting description of a beach by picking realistic examples of the people he saw and by describing them honestly. The description tells us clearly what he saw. Verbs such as the gulls *squawked* and the whole beach would be *aroused* are exactly the right words to convey their effect. They are not unusual or far-fetched but neither are they obvious.

'The sun was hot on my back as I picked my way along the crowded beach. The day was very warm and it had brought with it the usual families who always flock to the seaside on such days. There were elderly people sitting in deckchairs, laughing proudly at their grandchildren's efforts to paddle and make sand-castles; mothers and fathers playing with their children; a group of teenagers playing with a beach-ball, first on the beach, then in the water; and children carefully carrying buckets of water from the sea to fill up the moats round their castles. Further along the beach a group of donkeys were plodding gently along the sand, carrying on their backs young children whose parents were walking alongside, carefully ensuring that their children did not fall off. Nearby, an ice-cream van was playing a gay tune to attract people, while gulls squawked overhead, and every now and again the whole beach would be aroused by the sight of a ship on the horizon.'

A second example shows how to begin telling a story. The chosen setting is realistic and convincing—we can believe that the writer really did sit up with her mother after a power-cut. Also, the description of the quiet night and the flickering firelight puts the reader in the right mood for the ghost story that is beginning. The writer is making good use of a scene she knows well.

'One cold winter's night, my mother and I sat by the warm fireside in the lounge of our cottage. My father and brother had gone off to bed an hour earlier, owing to the fact that there had been a power-cut and the television was not working. Mother sat in her chair darning and I read by candlelight. The dancing red and orange flames of the fire lit the room with the help of two candles on the mantelpiece.
   ' "Isn't it strange, sitting here, sewing and reading by

candlelight?" my mother said rather unexpectedly.

' "Yes, I suppose it is," I replied, "but what made you say that, Mum?"

' "I was just thinking," she said; "I can remember the cold nights like this when I was in the Land Army during the war." '

The next example shows how the choice of the right detail and the right word makes the scene to be described seem romantically desolate.

'The old castle lies deserted on a peninsula among weeds and nettles with its broken walls beside it in a skirt of rubble, and the steps leading up to it rough and shattered. Weeds grow in every corner, mice scuttle here and there, and cobwebs hang from the remains of the rough stone roof. The courtyard echoes, bare and empty, its stones worn smooth by the feet of many people long dead. The great cannon lie, rusty and miserable, against the walls—forgotten.

'The great hall, where men once rejoiced with re-echoed laughter, is silent. Its massive doors groan reluctantly when they are opened, and floors creak as the ancient boards are walked upon. The towers lie in ruins among nettles and weeds in the sour soil below. . . .'

The last example is more humorous. Without attempting slapstick humour it suggests the startling experiences of the school-leaver who goes to a new college still being built.

'Having booked in at Reception, Ray walked over to the Dining Hall with two boys he had spoken to in the queue. The verges of the road were stacked with pipes, and on the car park fronting the Dining Hall, a cement mixer was competing with an auxiliary pumping set for the prize of being the noisiest engine in the building trades. Pushing through the entrance door of the Dining Hall, one of the boys almost fell over a workman still laying linoleum squares. Workmen seemed to be everywhere, light fittings were being put up, and a painter said, "Mind that door, the paint's still wet!" '

You will gain confidence and fluency from writing success-fully like this. If you write well about your own experiences, it will help you to write more imaginatively about other people's. It will also improve other writing you have to do about history or science, about the foreign policy of Disraeli or the nitrogen cycle. Those who can write good descriptive prose can also record facts clearly and concisely. Success in one sort of writing encourages and supports success in another.

Subjects to write about

1 A bonfire
2 My favourite tree
3 Things that frighten me
4 The brook
5 An animal that stays in my memory
6 Creatures I dislike
7 Saturday night
8 An event in our family life
9 She was jealous of me!
10 Parents talking about the good old days
11 Going up to 'the chippy'
12 A story: 'No one cared'
13 A tragic accident
14 A dream
15 A first date
16 Our most interesting neighbour
17 A visit to a power station or factory
18 Market day
19 The dodgems
20 Our street
21 The school bus
22 My brother (or sister)
23 'There is no point in work unless it absorbs you like an absorbing game'
24 Continue writing from one of these beginnings:

   (a) In summer the path is at its most friendly
   (b) I have a pet who has a great sense of humour and is very intelligent
   (c) I sat down among the sand-dunes and watched the seagulls wheeling over some mysterious object cast up by the sea

TEST 2

A Write a composition of about 450 words on one of the subjects below:

    1 Choose one of the following and suggest improvements:

        (a) British railways
        (b) laws concerning driving
        (c) yourself
        (d) facilities for teenagers to meet

    2 Describe a well-known beauty spot or a place of historical interest
    3 Accidents in the home
    4 Is it a disadvantage to be an only child?
    5 Write a letter to a friend recommending a travel book or biography that you have recently enjoyed
    6 Write a letter to someone about to start at your school or college, explaining some of the main features of life there and describing some of the best-known people there
    7 You have been given a sum of money to buy three gramophone records. Describe the ones you would buy and your reasons for buying them

B 1 Write one of the following letters, inventing suitable names and addresses:

        (a) Your Youth Club wishes to hold a flag day to collect money to keep itself alive. As its secretary, write to the editor of your local newspaper urging people to give generously
        (b) Write to a neighbour apologising for damage to his property and explaining how it occurred
        (c) Write to the editor of your local newspaper attacking or defending the proposal to create a shopping-centre from which vehicles will be banned

    2 Write a page, as for a guide-book, describing an island or a castle or a prehistoric site or a beautiful church

3 Write an article on Bird Migration, using some of the
ideas below and adding ideas of your own if you wish.

Spectacular distances covered by migrating birds;
swallows from the British Isles and even the Arctic
Circle winter in South Africa; swallows come to this
country from Russia. Many cross large stretches of
ocean. They migrate usually in large flocks, some by
day, others by night. How do they navigate so
successfully? Many young birds migrate inde-
pendently of their parents, e.g. it is known for a
few-months-old swallow to fly from England to
Natal and back next spring to its birth-place. Why
do they go so far? There is no need to do so for
equally suitable conditions could be found in
Mediterranean countries as in South Africa. The
How and Why of Bird Migration remains a mystery.
But there must be reasons for their long and arduous
journeys.

Section II   SUMMARY AND COMPREHENSION

Read the following passage and then answer the questions
on it. It occurs at the end of a book in which the writer
describes how he walked from Land's End to John o'Groats
(from the extreme south-west of England to the extreme
north of Scotland), avoiding roads as much as possible.

Part of the journey could certainly have been done more
easily by car, but it would have been an entirely different
journey. Roads are all more or less alike. Walking is intimate;
it releases something unknown in any other form of travel
and, arduous as it can be, the spring of the ground underfoot
varies as much as the moods of the sky. By walking the whole
way I got a sense of gradual transition from one place to another, a feeling of unity. The mosaic of my own country and
its people had become a sensible pattern. Memory now
acts like that little polished cylinder in the museum at Fort
William which puts together the fragments of the portrait
of the Bonnie Prince. But this had been achieved at some
cost.

Rain depressed me and mist I feared—mist on Dartmoor, on Kinder Scout, in the Cheviots above Redesdale and in at 15 least three places in Scotland where, on the high tops, there is the additional hazard of drifting cloud. Cloud is impenetrable. It brought me to a stop. Through mist I went on, perhaps unwisely, but with caution and faith in a map and a bearing. I feared only a sudden drop, a *creag*. There are no unpredict- 20 able drops that I know of in England.

Only on Dartmoor are there bogs that I would not willingly venture near again, at least not in a mist. They seemed uniquely and deceptively deep, but, through a combination of ignorance and good fortune, I managed to get 25 round them rather than across them. Those encountered elsewhere, especially in the southern Pennines and Scotland, could be easily avoided or occasionally walked through with no more than muddy knees. Probing showed that, marginally, at least, they were not deep. 30

During the trip I discovered that without making elaborate detours some of the country's most-talked-about bits of walking country are substantially impassable. This is particularly evident on the so-called cliff-top paths of Cornwall, on Dartmoor, Offa's Dyke and, to a lesser extent, on 35 sections of the Pennine Way where directions are, in places, miserably inadequate.

A walker expects hostility in the vicinity of military training grounds; it is understandable on the part of private landowners who, in places, have been obliged, reluctantly, 40 to let pedestrians through ancient rights of way. But it is wholly intolerable on the part of government agencies, such as the Nature Conservancy and the Forestry Commission, which, in areas such as Teesdale and the Border forest, have blocked the long-distance trail north. 45

The walker is a convenient symbol for those who run cosy conferences on the importance of preserving the countryside. He is tolerated; he is even encouraged if he keeps to a few well-trodden tracks from points of surveillance where he can be watched and warded. But the tracks are short and 50 discontinuous. In the bits in between the walker is still to a great extent on his own.

He is the declared enemy of keepers, both private and

those employed by municipalities, such as waterworks
authorities. And landlords of most of the big public houses   55
make it abundantly clear that a foot-borne man is as un-
welcome among hard-drinking, wheel-carried customers as
the gypsies are. This is nothing new. In 1782 a German
pastor named Carl Philipp Moritz spent six weeks tramping
from London to Derbyshire and back. In Britain, he says,   60
the pedestrian seems to be

'considered as a sort of wild man or an out-of-the-way being
who is stared at, pitied, suspected and shunned by everybody
who meets him . . . in England any person undertaking so
long a journey on foot is sure to be looked upon and   65
considered as either a beggar, or a vagabond, or some
necessitous wretch, which is a character not more popular
that that of a rogue. To what various, singular and
unaccountable fatalities and adventures are not foot-
travellers exposed in this land of carriages and horses?'   70

Open country is diminishing rapidly. Those bits with
any claim to distinction are protected, badly, by government
agencies. The flooding of Upper Teesdale showed that the
Nature Conservancy was not only powerless to save the
place, but failed to realize its intrinsic importance until too   75
late. The wrangle that ensued is wholly discreditable to
government, local authority and industry.

1 Explain in a short paragraph why he walked instead of
   driving a car
2 Explain in about 150 words what were the major obstacles or dangers that he met in his walk
3 Explain why the writer is critical of government and
   municipal agencies or authorities.

CHAPTER THREE

Informative Writing

Both industrialists and teachers of science and engineering have urged that all students, especially engineers and scientists, should improve their ability to write English.

Today there is an increasing amount of technical writing. If we buy a car, we read books and manuals on its maintenance. If a housewife buys a washing machine, she is given a booklet on how to look after it. If a factory uses a new machine, an engineer may have to write advice to other users, and before that the manufacturers may have had to write technical booklets for their salesmen on how to stress its usefulness. Many people have to write, and read, more pages of technical information than they ever write, or read, on other subjects. Those who write such informative English need to keep up as high standards of writing as anyone else.

They need to avoid ugly language because it repels the readers or distracts them from what is being said. The scientist and the engineer usually have to work in close co-operation with other people, going to talks, conferences and committee meetings, and having to write papers so that other people who turn up to these committees can study their ideas beforehand. Those who write these papers have to put their ideas in the right order, and help their readers draw the right deductions. If the technician can write well, he will find that others will be keener to read his papers and more willing to listen to his ideas.

The Australian scientist H. G. Andrewarth thinks it necessary to give the following advice on how to write well about science:

'The scientist who has made a discovery should be able to tell his colleagues exactly what he did, how he did it and what are the conclusions to be drawn from his work. The clear, concise writing that is demanded of a scientist does not come naturally but only after many trials and much practice. The young scientist should avoid the mistake of copying the jargon that characterizes far too much of the "scientific literature".'

By jargon he means the unnecessary use of technical terms, such as *allergic* or *dichotomy* when a plain word like *hostile* ot *split* would do better.

In writing to pass on information about science or some similar topic, avoid abstract nouns when you can. Instead of writing: 'Solution took place', say more simply: 'The crystals dissolved'. Do not use nouns as adjectives when these sound awkward, as in phrases such as 'fertility decline' or 'our language decay progress'.

Avoid long words that are pompous or vague. Do not say 'ablution facilities' instead of 'wash-basins', or 'entertainment value' instead of 'fun'. Say that people starve, not that they 'exhibit evidence of malnutrition'. Use short words such as 'press' instead of 'pressurise', and avoid fashionable words or phrases like 'the materials are in short supply'.

Do not pack too many ideas into one sentence or move on to a new topic or fact until your reader has had time to absorb the first. To do this you may need to include apparently unnecessary words or phrases in order to keep essential points from following too fast upon one another. If one fact follows too soon upon the previous one, especially if they are in the same sentence, then the reader may not grasp the significance of the first before it is swamped by the second. In particular, numbers and statistical information often need to be isolated from the text.

If you are going to tell an unintelligent messenger to fetch Bill Watkinson, you may go up to him and say: 'You know Bill Watkinson, the man who is going bald? Tell him I want to see him now.' Your opening words when you addressed him were not wasted; they help the listener to fasten his attention on the subject of Bill Watkinson before the important message is given. Similarly in writing you may need some introductory words to help your reader to fix his attention on your main topic.

In an examination, you may be asked to state the case for a particular proposition—that factory farms are cruel—or you may be asked to give both the arguments *for* it and the arguments *against* it. First of all, you have to think of the arguments that you are going to use. You are more likely to summon up these in the examination room if you have previously read discussions of these problems in newspapers or in books, and if you have listened attentively to responsible programmes on television or radio.

Having thought out your ideas, you have then to find words that express them clearly and persuasively. In this kind of writing, the essential virtue is clarity. Your English should be straightforward. Short sentences are usually better than long ones, but it is also preferable to avoid monotony in the style and structure of your sentences. They need to be varied and interesting as well as straightforward. Remember that when such an exercise occurs in an English paper, it is a test of your ability to write well, besides being a test of your ability to argue.

Consequently you need to give your writing a plan. If you are giving the arguments for *and* against a maximum speed limit of 70 m.p.h. on all roads, do not mix them up in a haphazard way. One method is to put all the arguments *for* such a limit in one paragraph, put all the arguments *against* it in another, and then to pass judgment on the matter in a third. Another plan is to state one argument from the point of view of someone advocating such a speed limit, and then to see what the other side say about the same argument—e.g. one side argues that crashes at very high speeds do more damage than crashes at lower speeds; the other side argues that crashes at high speed are surprisingly rare.

Dividing your arguments into paragraphs and presenting them in a logical order will help your reader to notice when you are moving on to a different argument. It will also help your reader to see which arguments you regard as most important. Sensible paragraphing makes both your argument and your intention much clearer.

You may need to help your reader to follow your argument. You may usefully begin by saying that you are going to present a familiar or an unfamiliar topic, that your material is going to be elementary or advanced, or that you are talking (to return to our example) about driving in all countries or one particular country. It may help your reader to see how much importance you attach to a particular point if you begin with some such statement as:

Last, but not least, . . .

A more important point is that . . .

A minor point, to be mentioned only briefly, is that . . .

The simple words 'however' or 'but' or 'although' prepare the reader for the idea that the next argument to be presented will be in some way opposed to the arguments already presented; but a word such as 'moreover' prepares the reader for an idea that will support previous ones. An introductory phrase such as 'Practical considerations demand . . .' or 'From the point of view of a mathematician' will prepare your reader for the argument to follow.

There are times when it is useful for you to state what is *not* your intention. For instance, if you are a geologist writing about the chemical properties of Rhodesian copper, it may be useful to say 'I want to ignore the political aspects of this topic.'

A problem in this type of argumentative writing is how much previous knowledge to assume on the part of your reader. Usually it pays in English Language to credit him with a little more knowledge than you would expect of him in other school subjects. It is probably best to suppose that your reader knows less about the subject than you do, but is not entirely ignorant of it. If you imagine a particular type of reader, with certain limitations but without complete ignorance, then it will help you to avoid both the mistake of saying what is obvious, and that of taking essential parts of the argument for granted.

To sum up—you are trying to present a case that will impress the readers who disagree with you or have not yet made up their minds, and to do this you must produce good arguments, include relevant evidence, and also appeal to your readers' emotions. You have to understand their probable reactions, and try to guide them in a particular direction. You need to understand, and to counter, the arguments that can be brought forward on the other side. You must not spoil your case by exaggerating it or by losing your temper; you must not think that all who disagree with you are fools or liars. Bring forward your arguments, but arrange them in an effective order, with facts and examples (possibly statistics too) as evidence to support your views.

B

TEST 3

A Choose one of the following, and write a composition of about 450 words:

    1 The beginning of a story in any setting you choose, introducing two of the main characters

    2 My ideal holiday resort

    3 Imagine you have moved into a newly built house with ample garden space. Describe how you would plan and prepare the garden

    4 Suppose you had to spend a month alone on an island with all your basic requirements supplied. What four or five things would you take with you to help to pass the time? Give reasons for your choice, which should be as varied as possible

    5 Qualities I admire in my friends *or* my friends' parents

    6 A disused mine or quarry or railway

    7 Look at the picture facing page 97. Write a composition on what it suggests to you

B   1 The publishers of a teenage weekly magazine offer a prize for a letter suggesting how it might be improved. Write a suitable letter

    2 Write a clear account of how to do one of the following well: look after one type of animal, make a dress, improve your performance at your favourite game or sport, clean the outside of a car, exclude draughts from the living room, plan a religious service for teenagers

    3 Choose one of the alternatives in one of the following pairs and state why you prefer it to the other:

        (i) a motor cycle or a scooter

        (ii) a holiday under canvas or a holiday in a caravan

        (iii) a house or a flat of equal size

    4 Prepare a brief guide to your town or village, or to a place of historical interest in it

Section II SUMMARY AND COMPREHENSION

1 Read the following passage and then write two paragraphs, one of not more than 60 words explaining the mystery which

the first Europeans found when they crossed the Pacific
Ocean, and a second of not more than 80 words explaining
how modern investigators decided that these South Sea
islands had been inhabited for a relatively short time.

When the first Europeans at last ventured to cross this
greatest of all oceans (the Pacific), they discovered to their
amazement that right out in the midst of it lay a number of
small mountainous islands and flat coral reefs, isolated from
each other and from the world in general by vast areas of sea.   5
And every single one of these islands was already inhabited
by people who had come there before them—tall, handsome
people who met them on the beach with dogs and pigs and
fowls. Where had they come from? They talked a language
which no other people knew. And the men of our race, who   10
boldly called themselves the discoverers of the islands, found
cultivated fields, and villages with temples and huts, on every
single inhabitable island. On some islands, indeed, they found
old pyramids, paved roads, and carved stone statues as high
as a four-storey house in Europe. But the explanation of the   15
whole mystery was lacking. Who were these people, and
where had they come from?
One can safely say that the answers to these riddles have
been nearly as many in number as the works that have treated
of them. Specialists in different fields have put forward quite   20
different solutions, but have always had their affirmations
disproved later by logical arguments from experts who have
worked along other lines. Malaya, India, China, Japan,
Arabia, Egypt, the Caucasus, Atlantis, even Germany and
Norway, have been seriously championed as the Polynesians'   25
homeland. But every time some 'snag' of a decisive character
has appeared and put the whole affair into the melting-pot
again.
We know with absolute certainty that the original
Polynesian race must at some time, willingly or unwillingly,   30
have come drifting or sailing to these out-of-the-way islands.
And a rather closer look at the inhabitants of the South Seas
shows that it cannot have been very many centuries since
they came. For even if the Polynesians live scattered over
an area of sea four times as large as the whole of Europe,   35

nevertheless they have not managed to develop different
languages in the different islands. It is thousands of sea miles
from Hawaii in the north to New Zealand in the South, from
Samoa in the west to Easter Island in the east, but yet all
these isolated tribes speak dialects of a common language   40
which we have called Polynesian. Writing was unknown in all
the islands, except for a few wooden tablets bearing incom-
prehensible hieroglyphs which the natives preserved on
Easter Island, though neither they themselves nor anyone
else could read them. But they had schools, and the poetical   45
teaching of history was their most important branch, for in
Polynesia history was the same as religion. They were
ancestor worshippers; they worshipped their dead chiefs
right back to Tiki's time, and of Tiki himself it was said that
he was son of the sun.   50
   On almost every single island learned men could rattle off
the names of all the island's chiefs right back to the time
when it was first peopled. And to assist their memories they
often used a complicated system of knots on twisted strings,
as the Inca Indians did in Peru. Modern investigators have   55
collected all these local genealogies from the different islands,
and found that they agree with one another with astonishing
exactness, both in names and number of generations. It has
been discovered in this way, by taking an average Polynesian
generation to represent twenty-five years, that the South Sea   60
islands were not peopled before about A.D. 500. A new
cultural wave with a new string of chiefs shows that another
and still later immigration reached the same islands as late
as about A.D. 1100.

2 Read the following short story (which for your convenience
  has been divided into three sections) and answer the
  questions following it.

A

   'My aunt will be down presently, Mr Nuttel,' said a very
self-possessed young lady of fifteen; 'in the meantime you
must try to put up with me.'
   Framton Nuttel endeavoured to say the correct something
which should flatter the niece of the moment without unduly   5

discounting the aunt that was to come. Privately he doubted
whether these formal visits on a succession of total strangers
would do much towards helping the nerve cure which he was
supposed to be undergoing. 'I know how it will be,' his sister
had said to him when he was preparing to migrate to this   10
rural retreat; 'you will bury yourself down there and not
speak to a living soul, and your nerves will be worse than
ever from moping. I shall just give you letters of introduction
to all the people I know there. Some of them, as far as I can
remember, were quite nice.' Framton wondered whether   15
Mrs Sappleton, the lady to whom he was presenting one of
the letters of introduction, came into the nice division.

'Do you know many of the people round here?' asked the
niece when she judged that they had had sufficient silent
communion.   20

'Hardly a soul,' said Framton. 'My sister was staying here
at the Rectory, you know, some four years ago, and she gave
me letters of introduction to some of the people here.'

He made the last statement in a tone of distinct regret.

'Then you know practically nothing about my aunt?'   25
pursued the self-possessed young lady.

'Only her name and address,' admitted the caller. He was
wondering whether Mrs Sappleton was in the married or
widowed state. An undefinable something about the room
seemed to suggest masculine habitation.   30

'Her great tragedy happened just three years ago,' said
the young lady; 'that would be since your sister's time.'

'Her tragedy?' asked Framton; somehow in this restful
country spot tragedies seemed out of place.

'You may wonder why we keep that window wide open   35
on an October afternoon,' said the niece, indicating a large
French window that opened on to a lawn.

'It is quite warm for the time of year,' said Framton;
'but has that window got anything to do with the tragedy?'

B

'Out through that window, three years ago to a day, her
husband and her two young brothers went off for their day's
shooting. They never came back. In crossing the moor to
their favourite snipe-shooting ground, they were all three

engulfed in a treacherous piece of bog. It had been that
dreadful wet summer, you know, and places that were safe in
other years gave way suddenly without warning. Their
bodies were never recovered. That was the dreadful part of
it.' Here the child's voice lost its self-possessed note and
became falteringly human. 'Poor aunt always thinks that
they will come back some day, they and the little brown
spaniel that was lost with them, and walk in at that window
just as they used to do. That is why the window is kept open
every evening till it is quite dusk. Poor dear aunt, she has
often told me how they went out, her husband with his
white waterproof coat over his arm, and Ronnie, her
youngest brother, singing, "Bertie, why do you bound?" as
he always did to tease her, because she said it got on her
nerves. Do you know, sometimes on still, quiet evenings
like this, I almost get a creepy feeling that they will all walk
in through that window. . . .'

She broke off with a little shudder. It was a relief to
Framton when the aunt bustled into the room with a whirl of
apologies for being late in making her appearance.

'I hope Vera has been amusing you?' she said.

'She has been very interesting,' said Framton.

'I hope you won't mind the open window,' said the aunt,
Mrs Sappleton, briskly; 'my husband and brothers will be
home directly from shooting and they always come in this
way. They've been out for snipe in the marshes today, so they'll
make a fine mess over my poor carpets. So like you menfolk,
isn't it?'

She rattled on cheerfully about the shooting and the
scarcity of birds, and the prospects for duck in the winter.
To Framton it was all purely horrible. He made a desperate
but only partially successful effort to turn the talk on to a less
ghastly topic; he was conscious that his hostess was giving
him only a fragment of her attenton, and her eyes were
constantly straying past him to the open window and the
lawn beyond. It was certainly an unfortunate coincidence that
he should have paid his visit on this tragic anniversary.

'The doctors agree in ordering me complete rest, an
absence of mental excitement, and avoidance of anything in
the nature of violent physical exercise,' announced Framton,

who laboured under the tolerably widespread delusion that   45
total strangers and chance acquaintances are hungry for the
least detail of one's ailments and infirmities, their cause and
cure. 'On the matter of diet they are not so much in agree-
ment,' he continued.

'No?' said Mrs Sappleton in a voice which only replaced   50
a yawn at the last moment. Then she suddenly brightened
into alert attention—but not to what Framton was saying.

'Here they are at last!' she cried. 'Just in time for tea, and
don't they look as if they were muddy up to the eyes!'

C

Framton shivered slightly and turned towards the niece
with a look intended to convey sympathetic comprehension.
The child was staring out through the open window with
dazed horror in her eyes. In a chill shock of nameless fear
Framton swung round in his seat and looked in the same   5
direction.

In the deepening twilight three figures were walking
across the lawn towards the window; they all carried guns
under their arms, and one of them was additionally burdened
with a white coat hung over his shoulder. A tired brown   10
spaniel kept close to their heels. Noiselessly they neared the
house, and then a hoarse young voice chanted out of the
dusk: 'I say, Bertie, why do you bound?'

Framton grabbed wildly at his stick and hat; the hall
door, the gravel drive, and the front gate were dimly noted   15
stages in his headlong retreat. A cyclist coming along the
road had to run into the hedge to avoid imminent collision.

'Here we are, my dear,' said the bearer of the white mackin-
tosh, coming through the window; 'fairly muddy, but most of
it's dry. Who was that fellow who bolted out as we came in?'   20

'A most extraordinary man, a Mr Nuttel,' said Mrs
Sappleton; 'could only talk about his illnesses, and dashed off
without a word of goodbye or apology when you arrived.
One would think he had seen a ghost.'

'I expect it was the spaniel,' said the niece calmly; 'he told   25
me he had a horror of dogs. He was once hunted into a
cemetery somewhere on the banks of the Ganges by a pack of
pariah dogs, and had to spend the night in a newly dug

grave with the creatures snarling and grinning and foaming just above him. Enough to make anyone lose his nerve.'   30
Romance at short notice was her speciality.

From Section A

1 Give the meaning of the following: self-possessed (l. 2), succession (l. 7), rural retreat (l. 11)
2 Why had Mr Nuttel called on Mrs Sappleton?
3 How did Vera mislead Mr Nuttel and make him believe her story?
4 What made Mr Nuttel think that Mrs Sappleton was not a widow?

From Section B

5 Explain the following: engulfed (l. 5), bustled (l. 23), directly (l. 29), prospects (l. 34), ghastly (l. 37)
6 In about 30 words sum up Vera's account of what had happened 'three years ago to a day'
7 How does the writer show that Mrs Sappleton found her visitor rather boring?
8 What sort of a person was Mrs Sappleton? Quote three words or phrases to support what you say
9 Why did Mr Nuttel find it 'all purely horrible'? (l. 35)
10 Explain in your own words 'laboured under a tolerably widespread delusion' (l. 45)

From Section C

11 Give the meaning of the following words: comprehension (l. 2), additionally (l. 9), imminent (l. 17)
12 In the paragraph beginning 'In the deepening twilight . . .' (ll. 7–13), why did the author use the words 'noiselessly', 'figures', and 'hoarse'?
13 Explain in your own words 'a chill shock of nameless fear' (l. 4)
14 How does the author make clear Mr Nuttel's way of leaving the house?
15 Comment on Mrs Sappleton's remark, 'One would think he had seen a ghost' (l. 24)

16 A dictionary gives five meanings for the word *romance*.
   They are
      (1) pleasing and idealised love-story
      (2) tender love-affair
      (3) non-realistic fiction
      (4) medieval tale of chivalry
      (5) glamour
   In which of these five meanings is the word used in l. 31?
   Write one or two sentences to justify your choice

From the whole passage

17 Quote or refer closely to three occasions in the story
   where Vera is shown to be a clever actress
18 Explain the meaning of the last sentence and justify it
   from two parts of the story
19 Why are Mr Nuttel's doctors' instructions humorous in
   view of what happens to him at Mrs Sappleton's house?
20 Write a brief paragraph to show that this story was more
   probably written sixty years ago than very recently

CHAPTER FOUR

Summarising

Why practise Summarising?

Most English Language examinations include an exercise in writing a summary. This used to be called by its French name of 'précis'; the differences between the two words are vague, but examiners now avoid the word 'précis' because it suggests adherence to formal rules (especially in insisting on indirect speech) which they wish to ignore. They use it as a test of your ability to understand what you have read. If you can pick out essential points, and then find your own ways of expressing them, you have really understood the passage.

The ability to summarise is very useful in a wide variety of occupations. If you are a journalist, you will have to choose the most important points in a politician's speech and reproduce them briefly. If you are a scientist, you may have to read a technical pamphlet on the operation of a new machine, and produce a shorter, simpler version for the less skilled staff of your firm. Whatever subject you study, you will have to make notes—a form of summarising.

General Points in Summarising

First you must read the passage carefully to understand its meaning; then, picking out the essentials, put the ideas expressed into your own words; finally you must write the answer in natural, fluent and readable English. Sometimes a summary of the whole passage is required; at other times you will be directed to summarise certain parts of the passage or certain aspects of it, and it is very important to read the question carefully and choose the relevant parts.

Studying the Passage

First, you must try to catch the general drift of the whole
passage by reading it through several times; make sure that you
grasp the main ideas, and also try to get a general impression of
its attitude and point of view. If it is arguing a case, which side
is the writer on or does he try to be neutral? Is the writing
wholly serious or occasionally humorous? Are certain ideas
emphasised more than others?

Having grasped the essentials, you must now re-read the
passage to see how well you have understood the details. It is
possible that when once you have identified the main ideas,
certain details that appeared unimportant at a first reading will
now seem more important.

If one section is more difficult than others, you may need to
read that part very slowly. The good reader, like the good
driver, is not the one who always goes slowly, but the one who
knows when to slow down.

If particular arguments in a passage seem to contradict one
another, take a closer look at them. It is unlikely that the
writer is deliberately contradicting himself; possibly he is
presenting both sides of an argument or suggesting that the
arguments on one side are weaker than those on another. He
may introduce the ideas that he does not really believe with some
slighting phrase, such as 'It could, of course, be argued . . .'
(meaning 'not by me') or 'Some people believe . . .' (meaning
'I am not so easily deceived'). In reading this sort of material,
you need to decide, early on, where the writer stands and
what his intentions are, but you must also be ready to change
your view if a closer reading of the passage produces facts that
do not fit in with your first theory.

Another problem in summarising is that you should omit
examples when possible. If the original passage is full of
tersely expressed ideas, each illustrated by an example, the
only way in which you will cut the original down to a third
is to cut out the examples ruthlessly; but sometimes the
author bases so much of his argument on a major example that
to leave it out altogether would make your answer too short.
So be ready to cut out examples when this makes summarising
easy; but do not apply this theory too relentlessly.

Notes and Rough Draft

The passage—or section—that you are required to summarise will have a certain number of main points. If you were summarising a passage about newspapers, your notes about the good done by newspapers might be something like this:

1 Newspapers are popular
2 The faults of some are not shared by others
3 They show their readers what the world is really like
4 They reveal faults in society so that these can be got rid of
5 Newspapers can educate young readers.

The first step in preparing to write a summary of a passage is to make brief notes, such as these, on its main points, section by section. You must include all the essential ones; for the examiner himself may be using this sort of list of main points, and may be giving you so many marks for each essential point you include. Consequently, if your list of points seems short, have another look at the passage to see if you have left out something important.

Using these notes, and referring back to the passage as little as possible, make a rough draft. In examinations you are always entitled to write this rough draft first; indeed when there is a word limit you should do so. But help the examiner by making it obvious that this is rough work; write your rough work in pencil and put an ink line right through it when you have finished.

In writing even this rough draft, you should use your own words as much as possible. You may well have to use *some* of the words of the original because they are the only possible ones to express what the writer has to say; for instance if you are summarising a passage about holiday *accommodation,* no other word will include every type of place where holiday-makers sleep, from a camp-site to the Grand Hotel. But avoid copying whole phrases from the original, for if you do this the examiner will suspect you of not understanding them; so if you repeat one of the original words, see if you can use it as a different part of speech; e.g. instead of using the noun 'accommodation', it might be possible to use the verb 'accommodate'.

You must summarise only the material in the passage

before you; you must not add your own ideas or comment on, or criticise, the ideas of the writer, even if you do not agree with them.

Sometimes you are faced with the problem of what tense to write your summary in. It used to be thought necessary to write in Indirect Speech, where all you wrote was dependent on 'The writer said that'. Verbs had to be changed into one tense further into the past, and changes had to be made to personal pronouns, adjectives, adverbs of time and place, and some other words. Newspapers still use this type of indirect speech when summarising speeches made by politicians. But examiners no longer demand this, although you may find it a useful way of dealing with parts of your summary.

Final Stage

Having written your rough draft, count the number of words used. If there are too few, look for essential points you have omitted. If you have exceeded the word limit, you must find ways of reducing the number by telescoping ideas or re-phrasing certain sentences more concisely; you will lose marks if you use too many words.

You must now re-read your rough draft, to ensure that it is free of errors of spelling and punctuation, and that it reads naturally and smoothly as though it were a piece of your own original composition. Write in complete sentences, and remember that your answer is judged as a piece of composition as well as a summary. Look carefully for ways of linking up your sentences to give continuity with useful linking words and phrases such as: moreover, although, in addition, never-theless, in consequence. Finally, when you are sure that your version has all these positive qualities, write out your fair copy and make sure you have cancelled the rough one.

TEST 4

Section I TOPICS FOR COMPOSITION

A   Write a composition of about 450 words on one of
     the following:

    (a) If you had the opportunity of travelling in a foreign
     country, which would you choose and why?

    (b) Suggestions have been made for the modernisation
     of your town or village. Consider the advantages
     and disadvantages of these possible developments
     and give your opinion

    (c) 'A world free from hunger'. Is this a possibility?

    (d) 'Safety First': 'Live Dangerously'. Which do you
     think is the better as a motto for life?

    (e) A day in the country or by the sea

    (f) An exciting adventure in an unusual setting

B 1 Write about 200 words on the following:

    You have been asked to contribute to a series of short
     talks on possible Youth Club activities and decide to
     speak on Pot-holing or some other outdoor activity.
     Write out your talk

   2 Write a letter on one of the following topics

    (a) To a local office of the Ministry of National
     Insurance enquiring about temporary holiday work

    (b) To a local newspaper protesting against the
     proposal to demolish a building of historical or
     architectural interest in order to build a new road
     or shopping centre

    (c) To your M.P. asking him if he will arrange to
     meet a party from your school or club and take
     them round the Houses of Parliament

Section II SUMMARY AND COMPREHENSION

1 Read the following passage and then answer the questions
  on it. In the juvenile court, a police inspector is giving evidence against Egbert Crump, but his mother, Mrs Crump,

tries to interrupt the proceedings. The 'I' who tells the story is a Child Care Officer.

'Your Worships,' began the Inspector. 'The facts in this case are as follows. The houses which comprise The Rat Yard are almost entirely let to sub-tenants, some of whom occupy only one room; and one of the rooms opening directly on to the Yard is so occupied by a Mr Simeon Wiss,   5
who is in fact a retired person living alone, your Worships, and a former ship's cook. This Mr Wiss owns a pet budgerigar which goes by the name of Shinwell.'

I saw Councillor Trotter's eyebrows give a sudden flap at this.   10

'Now, your Worships, Mr Wiss is in the habit of doing his shopping each morning, and if the weather is fine he is also in the habit of hanging the birdcage up in the open window of his room, so that the bird can catch a little sunshine while its master is at the market. This is, in fact, what occurred   15
on the morning of the 7th October, when Mr Wiss left his house to go shopping at approximately 10 a.m.'

Egbert was now concentrating on making a hole in his plimsoll by wiggling his big toe.

'It was with considerable concern and distress that Mr   20
Wiss discovered, on his return to his room at approximately 11 a.m. that same morning, that his bird was missing from its cage. He at first formed the opinion that the bird had in some way escaped from the cage and flown off, but observing that the patent door of the cage had been refastened, he at   25
length came to the conclusion that some person or persons had wilfully let the bird escape or had, in fact, stolen it. He instituted inquiries himself, which proved fruitless, and subsequently informed the nearest police station.'

Glancing at Mrs Crump to see if she was still attending, I   30
was terrified to find her gazing lecherously into my eyes, smiling and fluttering her eyelashes. I looked hastily at the Inspector.

'Now, at 11.40 a.m., the following morning, that is October 8th, your Worships, P.C. 515 Bowman was patrol-   35
ling his beat in Blight Street when he was approached by a gentleman who subsequently identified himself as Mr Wiss,

and who said to him'—(here the Inspector put on the ringing pontifical voice he always used when quoting somebody else verbatim). 40

'"Here, mate, them bleeding Crumps have swiped my budgie."'

'Cheeky swine!' observed Mrs Crump loudly.

'In response to the Constable's inquiries, Mr Wiss described what had happened the previous day, and added that he had 45 just returned from his morning shopping to find that a further offence had apparently been committed. The Constable's attention was then drawn to a large tin standing on Mr Wiss's window-sill, marked National Dried Milk but actually half-full of birdseed. Constable Bowman then observed that from 50 a point just outside the window, a thin but discernible trail of birdseed led across the Yard and in at the door of No. 6.'

Mrs Crump had raised her short legs, side by side, horizontally in front of her, and was now looking at them with one eye shut. 55

'Now, your Worships, I must now point out to you that this budgerigar, Shinwell, had been taught by Mr Wiss to talk, and had, in fact, become very proficient in the recitation of a bawdy verse which, I understand, commences with the words: "There was an old Bishop of Brighton." 60

'Your Worships, the Constable, accompanied by Mr Wiss, then followed the trail of seed into a basement passage-way below No. 6, The Rat Yard, where he observed three small boys, the accused and two others, leaning against the wall, whistling. P.C. Bowman inquired what they were doing, and 65 the eldest boy, Crump, replied to the effect that they were practising for the carol-singing season, as the Constable might have learnt had he washed his great cloth ears out. Upon P.C. Bowman making a slight gesture towards the boy, Crump recoiled in a guilty fashion, and a voice was 70 then distinctly heard repeating: 'There was an old Bishop of Brighton . . .' Constable Bowman then said: 'I am inquiring into the disappearance of a budgerigar, and I have reason to believe you can assist me in my inquiries.' The boy Crump then said: 'Oh, all right, here it is.' He was cautioned, and said: 75 'Yes. Poor little perisher, I only meant to let him free, as his cage was too small for him, but he would not leave me then,

so I had to go back and pinch the seed.' Crump was told he
would be reported for these offences, and he replied: "Right-
ho, bighead!"'   80

This concluded the facts of the police case against Egbert,
but there followed a rather boring interlude while P.C. 515
Bowman was led over the same story again to confirm its truth
on oath. When he had finished, the Clerk said that he could be
questioned on what he had said; Egbert had nothing to say,   85
but Mrs Crump was on her feet at once.

'I saw you an' ole Wiss 'avin' a drink together down at
The Dog, only yesterday,' she said.

Bowman blenched; this was true but, fortunately, the
Clerk diverted the question by saying: 'Mrs Crump, you must   90
ask questions about what the witness said, you must not make
statements at this stage, you know.'

This put Mrs Crump off her stroke for a moment, and she
lost the thread, but recovered to say: 'There was two other
boys wiv Egg when you knocked him off, why ain't they   95
'ere?'

The Inspector answered for Bowman by saying: 'Your
Worships, the two boys mentioned have both been inter-
viewed by the police, and it does appear that on the day
when the bird was taken, they were both in school.'   100

1 Explain in about 80 of your own words the main facts
  that point to Egbert Crump being guilty of theft
2 Indicate which features or details of this story are meant
  to be funny, and justify your choice
3 Choose two phrases that seem pompous and explain how
  they achieve this effect
4 Discuss whether there is any justification in Mrs Crump's
  attempts to suggest that her son's trial is an unfair one
5 Show how the writer suggests that the system of justice
  is trying to use a steamhammer to crack a nut

2 Read the following extracts from two different books, and
then answer the questions on them. Both deal with much the
same point in the story of the Spanish Armada, the fleet which
tried to attack England in 1588. Led by the Duke of Medina
Sidonia, it has been defeated by the English fleet and harassed
by a storm. It attempts to sail back to Spain round the north
of Scotland, and as it passes,the latitude of Edinburgh the
English ships break off their pursuit.

A

The wind held. The two fleets sailed northward, past the
height of Hull, past the height of Berwick. On the afternoon
of the fourth day, Friday, 12th (O.S. 2nd) August in about
latitude 56°N, the English turned away and headed for
the Firth of Forth, Howard was satisfied that the Spanish did   5
not mean to try for a landing, and food and water on his
ships was running out.
    From the poop-deck of the *San Martin* Medina Sidonia
watched the English haul into the wind and drop farther and
farther astern. He had hardly quitted his post there since   10
the first nightmarish battle off Plymouth almost two weeks
ago. Men had been killed all about him, a musketeer, a boat-
swain and some of the greatest gentlemen of Spain, but
except for a stiff leg from a gash in the thigh last Monday
morning he had remained unscathed. Now and then he had   15
gone below to snatch a little food or a few hours' sleep, but
mostly he had eaten or neglected to eat whatever was brought
him on deck, and he had stayed leaning on the taffrail through
most of the short nights. He leaned there now, watching
the wretchedly familiar topsails vanish into the west. He   20
wore only doublet and hose and short cape. He had given
his great boat-cloak to Fray Bernardo de Gongora, who
had brought nothing from the *Rosario,* and his other cloak
covered a wounded boy in his cabin below. It was cold.
Yet he stayed leaning on the taffrail long after the last topsail   25
had sunk from sight. If he had wondered sometimes, coming
up the Channel, whether the Armada was advancing in
triumph or fleeing from the enemy, there was no doubt now.
This was flight, even though the English no longer pursued.
This was defeat. He had done his best, and his best had not   30

been good enough. Perhaps an abler, more experienced man? Francis Drake had said he would make the Duke of Sidonia wish himself back at St Mary's Port among his orange trees. We do not know where the duke wished himself that night.

B

Drake thought they would perhaps make for the Baltic or some port in Norway. They would meet no hospitable reception from either Swedes or Danes, but they would probably try. One only imminent danger remained to be provided against. If they turned into the Forth, it was still   5
possible for the Spaniards to redeem their defeat, and even yet shake Elizabeth's throne. Among the many plans which had been formed for the invasion of England, a landing in Scotland had long been the favourite. Santa Cruz, the admiral whom Philip first selected to command the Armada but who   10
died before it sailed, had always preferred Scotland when it was intended that he should be the leader. Many officers in the Armada must have been acquainted with Santa Cruz's views. The Scotch Catholic nobles were still savage at Mary Stuart's execution, and had the Armada anchored in   15
Leith Roads with twenty thousand men, half a million ducats, and a Santa Cruz at its head, it might have kindled a blaze at that moment from John o' Groat's Land to the Border.

But no such purpose occurred to the Duke of Medina Sidonia. He probably knew nothing at all of Scotland or its   20
parties. Among the many deficiencies which he had pleaded to Philip as unfitting him for the command, he had said that Santa Cruz had acquaintances among the English and Scotch peers. He had himself none. The small information which he had of anything did not go beyond his orange   25
gardens and his tunny fishing. His chief merit was that he was conscious of his incapacity; and, detesting a service into which he had been fooled by a hysterical nun, his only anxiety was to carry home the still considerable fleet which had been trusted to him without further loss. Beyond Scot-   30
land and the Scotch Isles there was the open ocean, and in the open ocean there were no sandbanks and no English guns. Thus, with all sail set he went on before the wind. Drake and Howard attended him till they had seen him

past the Forth, and knew then that there was no more to fear. 35
It was time to see to the wants of their own poor fellows,
who had endured so patiently and fought so magnificently.
On the 13th of August they saw the last of the Armada,
turned back, and made their way to the Thames.

1 Analyse the different impressions that the two historians
  give of the Duke of Medina Sidonia
2 Choose two vivid phrases from each writer and show
  how they help to convey the writer's attitude to the
  Duke
3 To what extent do these accounts give more emphasis to
  Sir Francis Drake, a dramatic character, rather than to
  Howard, the English commander?
4 Explain the meaning of the following words as used in
  Passage B: hospitable (l. 2), imminent (l. 4), redeem
  (l. 6), shake (l. 7), savage (l. 14), conscious (l. 27),
  attended (l. 34).
5 What differences of fact can you find in these two
  accounts, apart from their different characterisations of
  the Spanish commander?
6 Choose three examples (from either account or from
  both) of how a short sentence is used for dramatic
  effect. Comment briefly.

CHAPTER FIVE

Understanding What You Read

The meaning of a word. As you read, you have to do several things at once. You should understand the meaning of the words in front of you, relate them to their context (that is, to the circumstances in which they are used), try to judge the writer's intention or purpose in presenting his ideas in a particular way, detect any irony that may be lurking below the surface, read between the lines if that is called for, and make deductions that are necessary to your purpose.

You need to understand the words you are reading, but this may be difficult. Firstly, you may not have seen the word before, or may not have seen it often enough to have a clear idea of its meaning. The more books you read for pleasure, the more likely you are to have met it before and to have some idea of what it means. Nevertheless, even if you have never met a word before, you should be able to deduce from its context what it means. For instance if you meet the word 'transmogrification' for the first time you ought to be able to tell from the general meaning of the sentence that this new word means 'change'. Secondly, a word may have several meanings and you need to see which is intended. When you read about a 'park' you need to see whether it is a private park, a municipal park or a car-park. When you read the word 'upright' you have to decide whether it means vertical or honest. When Kingsley describes the coast of Devon as 'a howling wilderness of rock and roller', you must not be like the G.C.E. candidate who thought this was a reference to 'a wild sort of dancing', for 'roller' here means a long, swelling wave.

Thirdly, a word may be used in a sense that is out-of-date. The 'switch' that Tom Sawyer's aunt had behind her back was a slender cane and not an electrical device. Changes in the meanings of words can be a serious obstacle when reading a play by Shakespeare, or the Authorised Version of the Bible. For instance, 'abuse' as a Shakespearian verb means 'to deceive', and 'watch' as a biblical verb means to keep awake. These are only two of many, many words that have changed their meaning with the passage of time. At different times *sophisticated* has meant (1) adulterated (2) naughtily artificial (3) attractively artificial (4) complicated.

Fourthly, a word may be used in a technical sense. A chemist gives a special sense to the word 'salt' and psychologists use words such as 'intellect' and 'drive' in a much more precise and limited sense than others do.

Fifthly, a word that is deceptively familiar may be used to express an idea that is unfamiliar or complicated or abstract, with the result that the apparent use of easy words masks the difficulty of the ideas. Among words that cause difficulty are 'peculiar' (in the sense of personal or distinctive), 'moral' (because what is immoral to one man is not immoral to another), and 'defence' (which includes the radar set or even the spy who reveals the enemy's plans as well as the guns that repel him).

Finally, a growing difficulty is that certain words such as 'gas' have different meanings in England and America.

The result of these various factors in the meaning of individual words is that your understanding of any extract depends on your grasping certain key words that the author has used to convey his essential meaning. These words may not be the longest or the most unusual. If you can understand these key words, you will be able to deduce the meaning of many that are new to you.

The writer's intention. Another important aspect of reading is that you must develop your ability to detect a writer's intention. He may be adopting a particular attitude towards his subject and seek to pass it on to you. He may have a definite motive in writing which leads him to present his material in a certain way. He may be trying to draw a moral from the evidence that he presents. It is important that you should develop a 'sixth sense' that will make you aware of the writer's intention.

When you are asked to answer questions designed to test your understanding of a passage, and even when you are called on to summarise it, you need to be sure that you are aware of the author's attitude to his subject. Some authors are objective—

that is to say, the writer is neutral and unbiased and presents
facts or ideas quite uncoloured by his own feelings. In other
passages the writer's feelings are obvious; he takes sides openly;
he tries to get his reader to share his own strong feelings and
to take the same side as himself. But at other times the writer
does not commit himself openly, and does not state his attitude
clearly. By *subtly* taking sides he expects you to catch from
his tone the same strong feeling of admiration or hatred that
he has towards his subject. In reading this sort of writing, you
need to decide to what extent the writer is suggesting praise or
blame, approval or hostility, by the words he uses. If we call
someone 'resolute' or 'obstinate', we are saying much the same
thing—that he was reluctant to change his mind; but 'resolute'
is the word we could use if we admire him and were praising his
stand for a good cause; 'obstinate' is the word that we would
use if we disapproved of him, and wished to suggest that he
was stupid to cling to a wrong idea. The Americans call such
words 'purr-words' or 'snarl-words'.

You have to read carefully passages that try to blame and
praise a person in turn. Let us take as an example the first
sentence that Sir Winston Churchill wrote about Hitler in his
book on the Second World War:

> Into this void (*i.e. Germany lacking anybody with real power*)
> there presently strode a maniac of ferocious genius, the
> repository of the vilest passions that ever corroded the
> human breast—Corporal Hitler.

The verb 'strode' suggests Hitler's energy and self-confidence;
'maniac' leaves us in no doubt about Churchill's fundamental
disapproval; the word 'genius' is an admission of Churchill's
grudging admiration of Hitler's abilities, but by describing it
as 'ferocious' he reminds us of the savage and brutal uses to
which Hitler put these abilities. Churchill next expresses
contempt in calling Hitler 'a repository'—a place where
unwanted things are stored; not content with condemning
Hitler's motives and aspirations as 'vilest passions', he compares them (by using the word 'corroded') to an acid eating
away the source of more generous emotions. His picture of a
hateful but formidable figure striding on to the stage of
German—and international—politics is then undermined by a

mocking anticlimax, reminding us that this man, who thought so highly of his military abilities, was merely a corporal in the First World War.

In reading such a passage, you must not expect the writer to give only one side of an argument; in this instance you must not assume that because this is Churchill describing Hitler you will hear nothing of the dictator's formidable abilities.

A further aspect of reading is that you need to understand the writer's ideas or to follow the way in which a string of examples or of subsidiary ideas is intended to illustrate or prove a major idea or argument. This will involve looking closely at what the passage or extract has to say. If a passage about telepathy states that experiments in telepathy produced results which 'were not impressive enough to convince the doubters', you may need to look closely again at it to see for certain what it says: it says that the experiments never proved that telepathy exists. You must be careful to distinguish between the actual idea in front of you and a similar idea you have gained elsewhere. For instance—to return to the example of telepathy—you might read about a man who goes abroad and dreams that he sees his father lying ill in an unfamiliar house; on his return he learns that his father died at that actual moment in a house like the one in his dream. You have to realise that this idea of dreams as a type of telepathy (the passing of messages from one mind to another without the use of the normal five senses) is quite different from the idea that dreams foretell the future.

The effect of context. Another important feature in comprehension is the effect of context on meaning. If we read 'The builder contracts to build a new house for a certain price', then, the surrounding words tell us that 'contracts' means 'agrees', and not 'shrinks'.

Of course, it may be a whole sentence, not just a single word, that is affected by its context. If a writer is arguing at some length about the need to build quite new accommodation for holiday-makers on a large scale, he may say simply 'New towns must be built'. In this context it may be clear that he is *not* referring to those new residential-cum-industrial towns that have been artificially built around big cities (as Stevenage and Crawley have been built to take some of London's surplus population), but means that *new seaside holiday towns*—new

Blackpools—must be built. At other times a whole paragraph may be meaningless unless it is read in close conjunction with a previous one.

Irony. Irony has been defined as a method of expression where the ordinary meaning of the words is the opposite of the real thought in the speaker's or writer's mind. If your friend treads on your toes, you may say, 'How *gracefully* you step!' You are saying the opposite of what you mean, and are using irony. In common speech we often call this sarcasm. But in writing you must distinguish more precisely between these two words. Sarcasm is irony plus malice or anger or bad temper or obviousness. If a writer keeps his temper in saying the opposite of what he means, this is irony.

A slightly more subtle form of irony is to use as a term of abuse or criticism a word that is usually a term of praise—or, in other words, to use a 'purr-word' as a 'snarl-word'. For instance, a novelist calls a profiteer 'law-abiding' in order to suggest that he keeps the letter, but not the spirit, of the law. In *Nicholas Nickleby* Dickens describes the cruel, deceitful school-master, Squeers, and his hateful young son:

> 'Am I to take care of the school when I grow up a man, father?' said Wackford, junior, suspending, in the excess of his delight, a vicious kick which he was administering to his sister.
>
> 'You are, my son,' replied Mr Squeers, in a sentimental voice.
>
> 'Oh, my eye, won't I give it to the boys!' exclaimed the interesting child, grasping his father's cane.

The word 'interesting' is usually a word of praise; but Dickens, in calling the sadistic Master Squeers an *interesting* child, is using the word with a tinge of bitterness and irony. He is suggesting that young Squeers should interest a student of sadists' mentality.

Another form of irony is pretending to agree with the arguments that you wish to ridicule and then presenting them in a deliberately exaggerated way.

In all examples of irony there is something incongruous about what you are given to read. There is a contrast between the apparent meaning of the words and the reaction that the writer hopes for from his readers.

TEST 5

A Write an essay of about 450 words on one of the following topics:

    1 A holiday town out of season
    2 Having to put up with brothers (or sisters, or cousins)
    3 Bargain hunting
    4 What 'pop' singers sing about
    5 A magazine or journal related to your future career or to your hobby
    6 Imagine that you win a very large sum in a football pool. Write about the difficulties, dangers, and inconveniences that might arise from the possession of so much money
    7 'Sport is being ruined by external pressures.' Discuss

B Write about 250 words on one of the following topics:

    1 A conversation between two sixteen-year-olds in which one explains why he (or she) intends to stay at school and eventually go to a university or college, while the other explains why he (or she) intends to start work at once
    2 Write one of the following letters:
        (i) To the editor of your local newspaper urging the provision of a new swimming pool or other such amenity for your area
        (ii) Applying for one type of holiday post at a holiday-camp which needs dance-band players, swimming-pool attendants and people to look after small children
    3 Describe one of the following: a book shop, a school library, a barber's shop, a lorry park early in the morning, a football ground just before the match starts, the scene of an archaeological dig
    4 As secretary of a school or college society, write a detailed account of a meeting for the Minute Book
    5 Write a clear description of the processes and materials involved in ONE local craft (e.g. carving, pottery, basket-making)

Section II SUMMARY AND COMPREHENSION

Read the two following descriptions of St Austell, in Cornwall,
and then answer the questions on them. The first passage is from
the St Austell Guide; the second is from a book about Cornwall
by John Betjeman.

A

ST AUSTELL with its picturesque villages and rugged cliffs—
reaching down to delightful beaches—lies midway between
Plymouth and Penzance. The town itself is exactly forty
miles from both places. It is an ideal holiday centre for those
who want to get away from the conditioning of contemporary   5
progress and production lines. Indeed, the whole of Cornwall
is just perfect for those who want to rest and relax with
natural folk who still live and work closely with nature in a
different world from that of the hurly-burly of office and
industrial mass-production.   10
    We won't say that Cornish folk speak exactly the same
language as the rest of the British Isles—far from it—but
they do understand basic English and you can travel the
length and breadth of the Duchy without a phrase-book or
a ready reckoner—or even a passport. Wherever you pause   15
for refreshment you can be sure of a better cup of tea and as
good a cup of coffee as anywhere on the Continent. Nevertheless the Cornish dialect is a fascinating one; perhaps the
best way to hear it at its natural best is a group of fishermen
as they tidy up their gear at the end of their day. They still use   20
the same phrases that were taken overseas in the days of the
Pilgrim Fathers and have since returned to us as American
'slang'. One outstanding example is the ever recurring
'sure 'nuff'—an expression still used today all over the
county in its original sense.   25
    We'd like to talk more about the 'language' a little later but
first we must dilate on the softness of the climate. Virtually
surrounded by water and bathed by the Gulf Stream,
Cornwall is several degrees warmer than the rest of the
country in the winter and similarly cooler in the blazing   30
heat of midsummer . . .

B

Tin at the enormous Carclaze tin mine two miles north of this town was worked here from the sixteenth century till 1851, when it changed over to china clay. That industry was started in the St Austell district in the late eighteenth century by a local landowner Mr Carclew and Josiah Wedgwood. China clay is a greasy grey substance found just below the soil here and is made of disintegrated granite and felspar. It is mixed with water and according to *Kelly's Directory* (1930) 'while held in suspension is pumped up and passed over a very slight incline, depositing in its passing all the heavy matter, after which it is further purified in washing pits and dried ready for use. The men employed in this industry work short hours, the average working day being 7 hours only; few young persons are employed.' Today many executives are employed as may be seen from the parked cars outside the various office buildings of the big china clay combine in the town. China clay is used for pottery, face powder, size, calico and shiny art paper, to name a few of its purposes. It prospers. So does St Austell. The narrow mediaeval streets of the old village on the steep slope above and below the church are quite unsuited to the heavy traffic they have to take. Like Liskeard, St Austell needs a plan to save what is left of it. This includes the church (Holy Trinity) whose fifteenth century tower of yellow Pentewan stone is carved on all four faces of its upper stages and contains niches with figures in the Somerset style. The view of this from the steep hill above the old manor house north west of the church is one of the prettiest that St Austell has to show. Inside, the church is dark and towny. It has barrel roofs in nave and aisles with carved ribs, a Norman pillar-type font and is dark. It was reroofed at the east end by J. P. St Aubyn in the '70's and redecorated in the '90's by G. H. Fellowes Prynne. The stained glass is late Victorian except for a fine window by C. E. Kempe in the Baptistry (1908).

On the height in the middle of the town an Italianate Victorian house (Polcarn) mercifully survives in 11 acres of handsome park and woodlands. South of the church is the White Hart Hotel, a granite-faced building with a room of

Regency scenic wallpaper, and an oil painting by Edward   40
Lear. The Town and Market Hall are simple Italianate in
granite (1844) and what was the Friends' Meeting House is
another granite-faced simple building. Mostly St Austell
has had to cave in to the chainstores and the china clay
combine's demands. But at PORTHPEAN in the Parish and   45
Tenarren beyond it, where A. L. Rowse lives, unexpectedly
the old Cornwall survives. Here are Cornish elms and fields
sloping to the sea and at Porthpean a charming beach under
a yellow stone cliff from which the long outline of Bribbin
Head with its red and white striped beacon may be seen   50
across the bay.

1 For what purpose did the writer of A (obviously an
  advertisement) include four of the following
  expressions: picturesque (l. 1), rugged (l. 1), contemporary (l. 5), rest and relax (l. 7), in a different world
  (l. 9), hurly-burly (l. 9), the softness of the climate
  (l. 27)
2 How does A show that the Cornish tourist industry is
  afraid that too many Britons will take their holidays
  abroad?
3 What points does A make in favour of holidays in
  St Austell?
4 What facts that a holiday-maker would wish to know
  does A ignore?
5 A dictionary lists the meanings of *softness* as (1) lack of
  hardness (2) malleability (3) tendency to cut easily
  (4) smoothness (5) mildness (6) avoidance of extremes of
  temperature (7) freedom from mineral salts (8) absence
  of dazzling brilliance. In which sense is it used in line 27?
  (Briefly justify your choice)
6 EITHER show that for a popular advertisement A contains a surprisingly large number of difficult words,
  and discuss whether the advertisement gains or loses
  by including them
  OR criticise the grammar or structure of the sentence
  beginning, 'Wherever you pause. . . .' (lines 15–17)

7 Betjeman, like the St Austell Guide, is writing for tourists. How different are A and B in their assumptions about their readers' intelligence, knowledge and interests?

8 Today the word *executives* is used very vaguely to refer to people earning large salaries. How vague or unusual is Betjeman's use of the word in line 15?

9 In what ways is B more critical or more frank than A in admitting the presence of industry and commenting on such things as traffic jams?

10 Discuss the relative effectiveness of A and B in making you want to visit a Cornish beach

CHAPTER SIX

Objective Tests of Comprehension

In the next few years examining boards will make more use of objective tests of comprehension, until these form about a third of each paper. You may be given a passage to read and then given questions on it similar to this one:

As used in line 11, 'nascent' means approximately the same as

A left-wing
B propagandist
C just beginning to grow
D highly obnoxious
E half-grown

On a separate sheet you may be asked to write down the correct answer:

C

Although you will need to write much less in answering this type of question you may have to spend more time reading and thinking about the passage and the questions. Such questions are called objective because the marking of your work is objective: i.e. there is only one correct answer, and it is most unlikely that there will be any doubt in the examiner's mind about whether your answer is right or wrong. (Of course if you obstinately disobeyed the instructions, or could not copy accurately, and wrote down 'just beginning too groe', the examiner might not accept the answer, but such cases are very rare.)

You will see objective questions in the later tests of this book, which illustrate various forms of them. Each question usually consists of a stem which asks a question or makes an incomplete statement. You then choose one from four or five responses which answer the question contained in the stem or complete the statement in it. The incorrect answers are called *distracters:* they must not be too obviously wrong or they will fail to distract the poorer candidates. Sometimes they are not completely wrong; they are merely less correct or less suitable than the correct answer. Among types of distracter to look out for are those which state things that are true but have not been said in the set passage; those which exaggerate, and so falsify, a statement actually made; those which use many of the words of the original passage but change its ideas; those which are part of the correct answer but not the whole of it; and those which contradict something stated in the passage.

The example quoted above, and referring to the word 'nascent', concerns the meaning of one word or group of words. Perhaps a third of the objective questions set are of this type. This will suggest to you the need to own a good dictionary (such as *The Concise Oxford Dictionary* or the *Penguin Dictionary*) and to think about subtle differences in the meaning of words. Note that the meaning of the word is the one that it has in its context; we have already stressed on p. 53 that a word may have several different meanings or shades of meaning and that you need to decide which is being used at a particular point in what you are reading.

Other types of objective comprehension questions require you to show that you know the contents of the passage and are able to identify the main idea or theme. You may need to be able to deduce the writer's attitude towards his subject or his purpose in writing. In addition, the writer's style or technique, the vividness of his descriptions, and the emotional response he hopes for, may also be the subjects of questions. For some questions you may have to distinguish between literal and figurative (i.e. metaphorical) uses of words. You may also be asked to identify aspects of the subject which are not dealt with by the writer or facts that he implies without stating openly.

There is argument over what part guessing plays in answering an objective item. If you do not know the answer and make a blind choice, you have one chance in four or five of getting the correct answer, so it pays to write down something in preference to nothing. But in practice you are unlikely to behave like this. You are likely to see at once that one or two of the distracters are wrong answers. This may leave you with the hard task of deciding between the two most probable answers. Even here you may be guessing less than you think, for unconscious mental processes may be guiding you.

But there is no easy way to prepare for answering such questions. If you read widely for pleasure this will equip you *indirectly* in all sorts of ways to answer such questions. When you meet in a newspaper (or a textbook) a passage you do not understand, pull yourself together and decide to re-read the passage carefully and slowly. This conscious practising will equip you *directly* for answering such questions.

TEST 6

A Write an essay of about 450 words on one of the following topics:

    1 A crowded beach

    2 Incidents in an unlucky day in the life of a bus-conductor OR a lorry-driver OR a farmer OR a shop assistant

    3 Prejudices (Discuss various kinds of prejudice, their causes, and possible cures)

    4 The pleasures of one of the following:
       pony trekking, cycling, sailing, fishing, photography, sketching, dancing

    5 In hospital

    6 Write the story of a lucky escape and imagine the events as occurring either before 1919 or after A.D. 2000

    7 Study the picture facing p. 128 and write a description of the scene it depicts, making relevant comments

B Write about 250 words on one of the following topics:

    1 Imagine that you have an elder brother or sister in Australia or Canada. Write a letter for this week, giving the news of home and school that you think will interest him or her

    2 You are a farmer and have a caravan to let. A group of young people has written to you asking for details about the caravan, about the facilities you offer and the safeguards you require. Write a reply to the secretary of the group

    3 You were the only witness of an accident in which a car swerved to avoid an animal and collided with another car. A lawyer asks you as an independent witness to make a written statement. Write a clear, accurate, detailed account of what you actually saw

    4 Write a report for the guidance of future purchasers of some mechanical or electrical device with which you are familiar, such as a bicycle, a sewing-machine, an electric drill, or a washing-machine. Consider its

good features and any faults it may have, its 'value for money', and whether you would or would not be pleased to recommend it to others

5 You have been asked to contribute to a discussion on 'supermarkets *v.* the small shop'. From the following notes, write out your contribution to the discussion. Supermarkets: convenience of 'one-stop' shopping—brightness and cleanliness of premises—low prices are claimed—no waiting to be served—loss of personal touch—impersonal—suspicion of indifferent quality of some goods—temptation to buy unwanted but attractively displayed goods—loss leaders.
'The corner shop': proprietor knows all his customers—quality always to be depended on—few cut prices—delays in being served—chance to meet local house-wives—cosy atmosphere—old-fashioned layout—not easy to see goods displayed—or prices.

Section II SUMMARY AND COMPREHENSION

1 Below are printed two accounts of the death of General Gordon, who was killed at Khartoum in the Sudan in 1885. Read both accounts and then:

   (a) Point out the five most striking differences in the physical facts as related by the two writers
   (b) Comment on the different attitudes towards General Gordon's character taken up by the two writers
   (c) Answer the objective questions printed after the passages, by writing down the letter that stands for the best answer

I

It was at this hour, just as day was breaking, that Gordon roused from one of those short and troubled slumbers which for months had been his only rest, quitted the palace and moved, at the head of a small party of soldiers and servants, towards the Church of the Austrian Mission (which had been   5 made the reserve magazine of the town).

Walking in advance of his party, which did not number

more than twenty men, Gordon drew near the church. From
the lost town, still lying in shadow to the right, the shouts of
a victorious enemy and the cries of a perishing people rose   10
in deeper volume of sound. Ere yet the little band of footmen
had crossed the open space between palace and church, a
body of Arabs issued from a neighbouring street. For a
moment the two parties stood almost face to face, then a
volley of musketry flashed out at close range, in the yet   15
uncertain light, and the bravest and noblest soldier of our
time was no more.

II

Early in the morning of the 26th, the Arabs crossed the
river. The mud, partially dried up, presented no obstacle;
nor did the ruined fortification, feebly manned by some half-
dying troops. Gordon had been on the roof, in his dressing-
gown, when the attack began; and he had only time to hurry   5
to his bedroom, to slip on a white uniform, and to seize up
a sword and revolver, before the foremost of the assailants
were in the palace. The crowd was led by four of the fiercest
of the Mahdi's followers—tall and swarthy Dervishes,
splendid in their many-coloured jibbahs, their great swords   10
drawn from their scabbards of brass and velvet, their spears
flourishing above their heads. Gordon met them at the top of
the staircase. For a moment there was a deathly pause, while
he stood in silence, surveying his antagonists. Then one of
them cried in a loud voice, '*Mala' oun el yom yomek,*' (O cursed   15
one, your time is come), and plunged his spear into the
Englishman's body. His only reply was a gesture of contempt.
Another spear transfixed him: he fell, and the swords of
the other Dervishes instantly hacked him to death. Thus, if
we are to believe the official chroniclers, in the dignity of   20
unresisting disdain, General Gordon met his end. But it is
only fitting that the last moments of one whose whole life
was passed in contradiction should be involved in mystery
and doubt. Other witnesses told a very different story.

1   'Lost' (l. 9) indicates that the town was already

    A out of sight
    B captured by the enemy

    C forgotten by Gordon

    D inadequately defended

    E ignored by its potential rescuers

2 By stressing that Gordon walked in front of his party the first writer stresses that Gordon was

    A rather rash

    B eager to become a martyr

    C somewhat impatient

    D in despair

    E a natural leader

3 In I all the following phrases imply that it was very early in the morning with the ONE EXCEPTION of

    A 'just as day was breaking' (l. 1)

    B 'roused from . . . short and troubled slumbers' (l. 2)

    C 'still lying in shadow' (l. 9)

    D 'almost face to face' (l. 14)

    E 'in the yet uncertain light' (l. 15)

4 The phrase 'a perishing people' (l. 10) suggests that

    A the defenders were trying to escape

    B the attackers were still killing the armed defenders and the unarmed civilians

    C the attackers were killing only the soldiers defending the town

    D the defenders were surrendering and laying down their arms

    E events were still hidden by night that had not fully ended

5 A clear example of how the language of this extract is comparatively old-fashioned and literary is

    A roused (l. 2)

    B slumbers (l. 2)

    C advance (l. 7)

    D shadow (l. 9)

    E uncertain (l. 16)

6 In the Church of the Austrian Mission (l. 5) there were stored

    A official papers
    B food and provisions
    C secret documents
    D ammunition
    E reserve soldiers

7 The second account is more

    A dramatic
    B factual
    C adulatory
    D credulous
    E straightforward

8 'Assailants' (l. 7) means

    A attackers
    B enemies
    C conquerors
    D foes
    E invaders

9 'Swarthy' (l. 9) means

    A brave
    B fanatical
    C dark
    D dangerous
    E villainous

10 One can deduce that 'jibbahs' (l. 10) are

    A big swords
    B armour
    C leather jerkins
    D religious oaths
    E long coats

11 'Surveying' (l. 14) means

    A assessing
    B confronting
    C inspecting
    D facing
    E defying

12   'Antagonists (l. 14) are
        A opponents
        B agitators
        C rivals
        D murderers
        E attackers

13   'Transfixed' (l. 18) means
        A killed outright
        B injured severely
        C grazed nastily
        D seriously injured
        E pierced completely

14   'Chroniclers' (l. 20) means
        A journalists
        B reporters
        C historians
        D eye-witnesses
        E spokesman

15   'Fitting' (l. 22) means
        A logical
        B probable
        C appropriate
        D likely
        E noteworthy

16   The second passage, in contrast to the first, makes
     Gordon appear more
        A foolhardy and vain
        B angry with his enemies
        C restless and on edge
        D indifferent to his fate
        E consistent in his ideas

17   The second writer thinks that Gordon's behaviour at the
      end

    A was admired by official historians
    B demonstrated his unpractical nature
    C was the only type of heroism possible
    D proved his belief in the Christian god
    E showed that he was arrogant and overconfident

18   The second passage makes the attack on Gordon seem
      more deliberately aimed at him personally because it
      stresses that

    A the city's fortifications proved ineffective
    B the leading attackers looked for him in his own
       palace
    C his attackers had only old-fashioned Arab weapons
    D like St Thomas à Becket he was attacked by four
       people
    E he was struck by several weapons

19   The two writers differ openly in what they say about
      all the following with the ONE EXCEPTION of

    A their relative beliefs in their own accuracy
    B the time of the day when Gordon died
    C the weapon with which Gordon was killed
    D the number of Gordon's assailants
    E the extent to which Gordon was aware of events
       elsewhere in the town

20   The first account, as distinct from the second, makes
      Gordon's death seem more of

    A an accident
    B an act of heroic defiance
    C a savage act of revenge
    D an act of racial antagonism
    E an unexpected surprise

2 ARE THEY PULLING UP OLD ENGLAND BY THE ROOTS?

Section A

Britain's hedges are disappearing fast. In the 1960s, there were
more than 600,000 miles of them. Now, they are vanishing at
the rate of 5,000 miles a year, with the pace of destruction in
Eastern England 10 times as fast as it is in the rest of the
country.   5

Hedges have existed in England since Anglo-Saxon times,
that is, for at least 1,000 years. Some originated as parish
boundaries, others from sticks pushed into the ground to
become the living fences that are such a feature of our
landscape. Ancient hedges in Britain account for only a small   10
proportion of the whole, and there is a growing movement
for their preservation as ancient monuments.

These old medieval hedges are often the ones winding
along a circuitous roadside, perhaps once a parish boundary.
They have a greater variety of bush growth, plant and insect   15
life than the hawthorn hedges, which date mostly from the
enclosure movement of the eighteenth century, and which
are usually straight field-dividers

Their purpose, through the Enclosure Acts, was to keep
things in or to keep things out, and they helped farmers to   20
get on with the selective breeding of animals and growing of
crops. But there was an outcry about the coming of hedges
then, just as there is concern about their disappearance
now.

Section B

The pattern of farming of which hedges were an integral
part gave our landscape its green, deceptively tree-covered
look compared with the boring, open stretches of European
farmland. Cattle, horses and sheep needed hedges for shelter
and shade. A horse team could not plough more than a five   5
acre field in a day so there was no point in fields being much
bigger.

Now, a tractor can cover 50 acres in the same time.
Hedges get in the way, push up costs, so they must go.
In arable areas like East Anglia and Lincolnshire, where   10

prairie farming is getting a grip, there are fewer farm animals about and so little need for shelter. Farmers say hedges take up too much land, harbour pests and weeds, cause crops in their shade to grow unevenly and cost too much to maintain. 15

Conservationists argue, on the other hand, that trees make up a sizeable part of the hedgerows, with oak, ash and elm predominant. But mechanical trimming of hedges and the arbitrary lopping of young saplings is causing great havoc and many hedgerow trees are becoming rare, especially the 20 English elm.

The balance of nature is upset. Well-hedged land can support up to 1,000 pairs of birds on every 1,000 acres, because hedges contain everything that the birds need, from nesting sites to food. Thousands of the 20,000 species of 25 insect life in Britain find shelter in hedges. The hawthorn is food for more than 80 kinds of butterfly and moth. Hedges are homes for rodents on which hawks and owls feed. The vanishing hedge is one of the reasons why there are fewer partridges. 30

The Ministry of Agriculture gives grants to farmers who want to clear their hedges. It gives grants to those who want to keep them, too, but preservationists say it is the clearance grants which get promoted. The Ministry denies partiality. It says it allows grants for the removal of hedges or to plant 35 wind-breaks under the Farm Improvement Scheme solely on the needs of the individual farm.

Section C

Wind erosion can be a serious problem in Eastern England, but it is not all the fault of the disappearance of hedges. In places like the Black Fen, where wind-blows are an annual problem, there have never been hedges, only dikes; but 12-ft willow hedges are now being introduced as one solution 5 to the special problem of the fens.

Farmers are also using other barriers to trim wind speeds and protect crops. They plant rows of barley or use hessian screens. Experiments are even being made with plastic mesh, and irrigation is being used to make the light soil particles 10 stick together. From a farming and economic point of view, these are admittedly better bets than hedges.

Farmers complain that there is a lot of alarmist talk about vanishing hedges and soil erosion. Views on the efficiency of hedges vary. Mr Michael Darke, secretary of the Parlia-   15 mentary committee of the National Farmers' Union, put a rural perspective on the conservationist anguish over hedges. 'A lot of urban people who have got a kind of half-memory about the countryside from previous generations come into the country and suddenly become terribly concerned about its   20 appearance and what the farmer is doing The pattern of farming has always created the landscape, and what the farming community is doing now is sculpting a new landscape.'

It is often forgotten that farming largely created the   25 hedges, and the thought that some farmers chop down trees and hedges in the mistaken idea that they are tidying up the countryside can be dismissed.

Moreover, there is every sign that hedge destruction is over the peak. Farmers who want fields big enough to fit modern   30 machinery now have them. Machinery will not get much bigger because it gets heavier and causes compacting of the soil. 'We have got to start considering positive plans for tree-planting and encouraging farmers to plant up odd corners of their land with trees,' said Mr Darke. 'A lot of   35 farmers are pretty sentimental—there is no malice intended towards the landscape or wildlife.'

Section A

1 The oldest type of hedge has all the following character-istics EXCEPT ONE. Which? It

   A is at least 1,000 years old
   B was often created as a boundary between two
       parishes
   B is much rarer than the other type of hedge
   D protects a comparatively large variety of bushes
       and insects
   E divides fields in a comparatively straight line

2 The other type of hedge

    A often follows a winding road around the boundaries of a village

    B was intended to keep certain animals away from crops and other animals

    C was built in response to a popular demand from a large majority of the people

    D produced uninteresting open areas of farmland

    E was used, almost entirely, to aid the growing of crops rather than the rearing of animals

3 'Circuitous' (l. 14) means

    A roundabout

    B indirect

    C winding

    D devious

    E circular

4 The word 'concern' (l. 23) shows that when many people see the partial disappearance of hedges they

    A are just not interested

    B become emotional

    C feel anxiety

    D show exaggerated fears

    E experience disappointment

Section B

5 'Integral' (l. 1) means

    A historical

    B original

    C essential

    D logical

    E natural

6 Which one of the following statements about Section B is not true?

    A it deals mostly with the present rather than the past

    B it consistently takes the ruthless line that hedges must go

C it says virtually nothing about economic reasons
for keeping hedges

D it has little to say about the hillier parts of Great
Britain

E it regrets the decline in the number of hedgerow trees

7 The word that communicates the strongest criticism of
modern farming methods is

A 'deceptively' (l. 2)
B 'prairie' (l. 11)
C 'mechanical' (l. 18)
D 'arbitrary' (l. 19)
E 'vanishing' (l. 29)

8 The reasons why hedges are sometimes destroyed
include all the following with the ONE EXCEPTION
of the idea that

A a tractor can plough a much larger field in one day
than a horse could

B hedges put up the cost of agriculture

C in some districts there are fewer farm animals
needing hedges for shelter

D East Anglia and Lincolnshire are adopting arable
farming for the first time

E hedges take up too much land and shade crops
near to them

9 'Predominant' (l. 18) means most

A popular
B powerful
C competitive
D numerous
E influential

10 'The balance of nature is upset' means that

A population grows faster than food production
B hedges provide birds with nests and food
C the absence of hedges robs birds and other
creatures of all that they need
D plants and animals are changing their nature
E hedges support a great variety of insects and animals

11   All the following are put forward as arguments for
     retaining hedges today, with the ONE EXCEPTION of
     the idea that they

    A make the landscape more green and interesting
    B provide shelter and shade for the cattle, horses
       and sheep
    C could support a comparatively large number of
       birds
    D preserve, directly and indirectly, a variety of
       insects, birds and animals
    E protect farmhouses from the wind

12   The Ministry of Agriculture claims that in the matter of
     hedges it

    A rightly helps farmers to remove hedges
    B considers the needs of those who want to preserve
       hedges as well as of those who want to remove
       them
    C gives too much emphasis to them as the only
       type of wind break
    D does not trust the individual farmer to judge
       the needs of his own farm
    E regrets the harm done to birds such as partridges

13   'Partiality' (l. 34) means

    A indifference
    B callousness
    C inconsistency
    D dishonesty
    E bias

Section C

14   The blowing away of top soil by the wind

    A is chiefly due to the destruction of hedges
    B is an especially serious danger in eastern England
    C cannot be prevented by growing barley
    D drives farmers to spend a lot of money on expensive
       windbreaks
    E occurs in some years but not in others

15 Section C makes all the following points to show that
    sometimes hedges are introduced or preserved, with the
    ONE EXCEPTION of the idea that

    A willow hedges are being developed in the fens for
       the first time
    B various new types of barrier can prevent soil erosion
    C the climax of hedge destruction has passed
    D machines, and therefore fields, are unlikely to grow
       any larger
    E few farmers are keen to preserve the landscape

16 All the following words are used metaphorically
    (i.e. figuratively) with the ONE EXCEPTION of

    A 'trim' (l. 7)
    B 'screens' (l. 9)
    C 'bets' (l. 12)
    D 'sculpting' (l. 23)
    E 'peak' (l. 30)

17 Which of the following is NOT given as a reason why
    the destruction of hedges is slowing down?

    A most farmers who want bigger fields have now got
       them
    B farm machines are not likely to grow in size
    C farmers themselves are becoming more interested
       in planting trees
    D farmers think that hedges make the landscape
       untidy
    E farmers have no wish to destroy the wildlife
       whom hedges protect

18 On the whole, Section C of the article views the effects
    of destroying hedges as

    A very serious
    B quite trivial
    C much exaggerated
    D merely a matter of aesthetics
    E necessitating government action

19 Which of the following comments about punctuation is
     NOT true?

   A the comma before 'but' (ll. 1–2) helps to underline
      the contrast between the two halves of the
      sentence
   B the comma before 'only' (l. 4) might very well
      have been replaced by a dash
   C a semi-colon after 'hedges' (l. 26) instead of a
      comma might usefully have emphasised the
      contrast between the two halves of the sentence
   D the phrase 'who want fields big enough to fit
      modern machinery' does not have any commas
      because it defines which farmers the sentence
      refers to (ll. 30–1)
   E the dash after 'sentimental' (l. 36) introduces an
      emphatic repetition of what has been said before

20 Farmers

   A experiment with various barriers to protect crops
      from wind
   B think hedges make the countryside look untidy
   C complain that much talk of soil erosion under-
      estimates the danger from it
   D are missing the chance to create a new type of
      landscape
   E cannot be persuaded to plant trees for emotional
      reasons

21 Conservationists are considered in this article (e.g.
     Section B, 16) as people who wish to preserve the
     countryside's

   A animals
   B soil
   C beauty
   D fertility
   E productiveness

Other Questions

1   Write in under 120 words the main reasons which this
    author mentions in favour of preserving hedges
2   By referring to different points which the writer makes,
    show that she tries hard to give an unbiased expression
    of both sides of the argument

CHAPTER SEVEN

Letter-Writing

In examinations as in real life you may need to write two different types of letter. One is a letter to a friend; the other is a formal letter.

We will discuss the formal letter first. In writing this it is safer to include the conventional layout in full. Some parts of this still have an obvious usefulness in business correspondence; other parts are merely good manners. You disconcert your correspondent if you do not preserve the usual formalities.

The following example (with the lines numbered) will remind you of the orthodox layout.

Hillside,	1
12, Longtown Road,	2
Sutton,	3
Co. Durham.	4
10th June, 1976	5
Dear Mr Jones,	6
I should be grateful if you would let me know the name	7
and address of the manufacturer of the thermostatic fan which	8
you fitted to my Standard Triumph 2000 car (FFR 229J)	9
when I bought it from you in March this year. I need to know	10
this address so that I can order a replacement now that I have	11
moved away from your district.	12
Yours sincerely,	13
A. Smith	14
S. Jones, Esq.,	15
Manager,	16
Messrs Greenways' Garage,	17
Whitegate Street,	18
Newtown,	19
Easthamptonshire.	20

1. Do not put your name at the head of your address. Do not put inverted commas round the name of your house.

Nowadays you can present your own address in several ways, but you must be consistent, and keep wholeheartedly to one method. The usual way in the past was to indent the address so that each line began further to the right than its predecessor did, and then to put a comma after each line (except the last, which has a full-stop). This method is still correct, but you may receive letters where the writer's own address is not indented and/or has no punctuation at all: you may adopt this style if you wish, but if you do so, you must adopt it thoroughly.

5. There are many ways of writing the date, but the method printed on line 5 seems the best on a formal occasion.

6 & 13. When you are writing to someone whom you have never met, and with whom you have not had much correspondence, you address him as 'Dear Sir,' and you end 'Yours faithfully'. When you feel you have got to know him, even if it is only through letters, you may address him as *Dear Mr Jones*. Your ending of the letter must match your beginning. If you begin *Dear Sir,* you must end *Yours faithfully* or *Yours truly*. If you begin *Dear Mr Jones,* you must end *Yours sincerely*. Note that *sincerely* and *faithfully* begin with a small letter. There are more servile and elaborate ways of ending a letter besides *Yours faithfully* and *Yours sincerely,* but they are better avoided.

14. If you are a woman, it will be helpful to put *Miss* or *Mrs* in brackets *after* your signature.

14 & 15. It is usual in writing formally to be more polite to other people than to yourself: e.g. you refer to yourself as *A. Smith,* but to your addressee as *S. Jones, Esq.*

15–20. It is usual to include the address of the person you are writing to. Sometimes this is simply a polite gesture; at other times it may help a clerk to file the duplicate copy of the letter in the appropriate file. If you are writing to a firm containing the name of more than one person, then you address them as *Messrs:* e.g. Messrs Jones, Tomkins, and Ramsbottom, and you begin your letter *Dear Sirs*.

It is usual not to indent the name and address of the person to whom the letter is addressed. You may please yourself whether you write it above or below the main body of the letter.

If you are asked in an examination to write a letter to the editor of a newspaper, it is safer to include the full layout of a formal letter, and not the abbreviated layout that would probably be printed by the newspaper. Address it to the Editor and begin 'Dear Sir'.

Some letter-writers try to impress their readers by using stilted phrases that are often called 'commercialese'. They begin *We beg to acknowledge receipt of your esteemed favour of the 20th ult.* and they end *Thanking you in anticipation.* Such pompous phrases are meaningless and ridiculous, and do not have the effect that is hoped for. Avoid them.

In writing a letter in an examination you should be sure you include some precise facts or some worthwhile arguments. In other words, you ought to make several serious points. For instance, if you are asked to write to a theatre for tickets, you should make it clear what date you and your party want them for, in which part of the theatre you wish to sit, and perhaps which performance you prefer. If you are told to ask for cheap rates you need to explain your grounds for asking this: e.g. that you are all still at school, and that you form a large party.

Let us suppose that you are asked to write a letter attacking or defending the proposal to create a shopping precinct from which all vehicles are banned. If you wish to defend it you would need to put forward *several* arguments in its favour— that it will reduce road accidents to pedestrians; that it will help older people to shop at their leisure; that it helps young married women with prams and children to shop safely and pleasantly; that this plan has already proved successful in Coventry and other towns. You ought also to show that some of the arguments *against* the idea are less powerful than they seem; you need to show that special arrangements can be made for lorries delivering goods or for disabled motorists wishing to shop. It will help you to make points of this sort in an examination letter if you manage to imagine yourself in the circumstances that the question suggests. Try to put yourself in the shoes of someone who has to write the required sort of letter in real life.

In this sort of writing you must adopt the right tone. If you are asking for something, sound polite but do not be servile. For instance, if you are writing to ask a firm to mend your watch under the terms of a guarantee you should write as though you were confident they will do this, but should not be aggressively over-confident or demanding. On the other hand, do not lay your politeness on with a trowel. Be tactful and try to imagine the relationship between you and the person you are writing to.

It usually seems unreal when you are asked in an examination to write a letter to a friend or relative. Since the examiner wants to see whether you can write correct and interesting English, you have to be more correct and grammatical than you probably would be in writing to a friend in real life. So you must not use much slang or many slovenly expressions, yet you must avoid too formal a layout for the letter and must avoid too starchy a style in writing it. You might make sensible use of abbreviations such as *I've* or *I'm*. Try to mention recent events in your life that will interest the person you are writing to. Indeed it will help you to write appropriately if you think of an actual friend in real life and write what will appeal to him or her. Often it is the little details you include that will seize your friend's attention.

If you are writing as if to a friend or relative, do not make your layout inappropriate. In such a letter, do not include the name and address of the person written to; end with *Yours sincerely* or *Yours affectionately*, never with *Yours faithfully*. Avoid the common fault of ending your letter with an incomplete sentence, e.g. *Hoping to see you again soon*; you should make it into a complete statement, such as *I look forward to seeing you again soon*.

TEST 7

Section I TOPICS FOR COMPOSITION

A Write an essay of about 450 words on one of the following topics:

    1 The house I should like to live in

    2 A place with which you are familiar as it might have appeared in an earlier century

    3 A journey by river

    4 Friendship

    5 You have been promised a sum of money to spend on a holiday, and find that this will be sufficient for the cost of (a) one week with a conducted party to a foreign country, or (b) two weeks at a well-known holiday camp near a seaside resort in your own country or (c) three weeks on a farm in the British Isles. Discuss the possibilities and make your choice

    6 Write a story ending with 'I shall certainly not miss the chance of another adventure like that'

    7 Write a story or a description or an essay of comments suggested by any newspaper cartoon chosen by you

B Write about 250 words on one of the following topics:

    1 You have been asked to speak at a meeting of your Hobbies Club and have chosen to speak on 'Skating'. From a reference book, you make the following notes. From these notes write your talk.

Outdoor ice-skating rarely possible in Britain. British always keen skaters. In recent years indoor rinks opened. Now skating possible all the year. Ice-skating useful as a recreation. Good for health. Many competitions and championships, national and international. Another form of skating is roller-skating. Originally a substitute for ice-skating before indoor rinks. Now sport in its own right. Both forms of skating used for ice-hockey. Originated in Canada. Six in a team. Never very popular in England. Skating covers a series of recreations. Some enthusiasts take part in more than one. Learning to skate is not difficult. Strong ankles, good sense of balance needed. Most easily learnt when young.

2 You are to be the chairman at a meeting at which Major
G. E. Jones is to speak on 'Some Narrow Escapes'. In order
to introduce him, you find the following facts about him.
Study them, select what is suitable, and write your speech.

Born 1906. Educated at Easton School, Oxbridge University.
B.A. 1927. Worked in father's London office 2 years. Joined
Grenadier Guards 1929. Served in India and the Middle
East. 1934 Expedition to Greenland. 1936 in Canada with a
Business Mission. 1939–45 again served in the Army. Had
distinguished career in North Africa, Italy and France. M.C.
1943. D.S.O. 1944. In Berlin in 1948 during the crisis. Instructor
Sandhurst 1949–52. Member of Government Mission in the
Middle East 1954–5. Retired 1958. Very popular as a speaker.
Noted for stories of narrow escapes in war and peace. Publi-
cations: *Greenland Adventure,* 1935; *Germany in Peace and War,*
1949. *Adventure Unlimited,* 1959. Recreations: Golf, Shooting,
Photography.

3 Write a letter in one of the following sets of circumstances:

    (a) You have promised to help at a function for a charity
       in which you are interested, but shortly before the date
       of the function, you find yourself unable to go. Write
       a suitable letter of apology and explanation to the
       organiser

    (b) You have advertised your house for sale, and have
       received a reply from a Mr J. Smith, 17 St John's Road,
       Barchester, Wessex. Write to him giving full details of
       the house, its situation and amenities

Section II SUMMARY AND COMPREHENSION

1 Read the following description of a chimpanzee and then
write two paragraphs:

    (a) in 100 words showing how human Chumley seemed
    (b) in 70 words showing which features of Chumley's ap-
       pearance and behaviour surprised the narrator most

Cholmondeley, known to his friends as Chumley, was
a full-grown chimpanzee; his owner, a District Officer, was

finding the ape's large size rather awkward, and he wanted
to send him to London Zoo as a present, so that he could visit
the animal when he was back in England on leave. He wrote
asking us if we would mind taking Chumley back with us
when we left, and depositing him at his new home in
London, and we replied that we would not mind at all.
I don't think that either John or myself had the least idea
how big Chumley was: I know that I visualised an ape of
about three years old, standing about three feet high. I
got a rude shock when Chumley moved in.

He arrived in the back of a small van, seated sedately in a
huge crate. When the doors of his crate were opened and
Chumley stepped out with all the ease and self-confidence of
a film star, I was considerably shaken, for, standing on his
bow legs in a normal slouching chimp position, he came up
to my waist, and if he had straightened up, his head would
have been on a level with my chest. He had huge arms, and
must have measured at least twice my measurements round
his hairy chest. Owing to bad tooth growth both sides of his
face were swollen out of all proportion, and this gave him
a weird pugilistic look. His eyes were small, deep-set, and
intelligent; the top of his head was nearly bald owing, I
discovered later, to his habit of sitting and rubbing the
palms of his hand backwards across his head, an exercise
which seemed to afford him much pleasure and which he
persisted in until the top of his skull was quite devoid of
hair. This was no young chimp as I had expected, but a veteran
of about eight or nine years old, fully mature, strong as a
powerful man, and, to judge by his expression, with considerable experience of life. Although he was not exactly
a nice chimp to look at (I had seen more handsome), he
certainly had a terrific personality: it hit you as soon as you
set eyes on him. His little eyes looked at you with a great
intelligence and there seemed to be a glitter of ironic laughter
in their depths that made one feel uncomfortable.

He stood on the ground and surveyed his surroundings
with a shrewd glance, and then he turned to me and held out
one of his soft, pink-palmed hands to be shaken with
exactly that bored expression that one sees on the faces of
professional hand-shakers. Round his neck was a thick chain,

and its length drooped over the tailboard of the lorry and
disappeared into the depths of his crate. With an animal of
less personality than Chumley, this would have been a sign of   45
his subjugation, of his captivity. But Chumley wore the
chain with the superb air of a Lord Mayor; after shaking
my hand so professionally, he turned and proceeded to
pull the chain, which measured some fifteen feet, out of his
crate. He gathered it up carefully into loops, hung it over one   50
hand, and proceeded to walk into the hut as if he owned it.
Thus, in the first few minutes of arrival, Chumley had
made us feel inferior, and had moved in, not, we felt, because
we wanted it, but because he did. I almost felt I ought to
apologise for the mess on the table when he walked in.   55

He seated himself in a chair, dropped his chain on the
floor, and then looked hopefully at me. It was quite obvious
that he expected some sort of refreshment after his tiring
journey. I roared out to the kitchen for them to make a
cup of tea, for I had been warned that Chumley had a great   60
liking for the cup that cheers. Leaving him sitting in the chair
and surveying our humble abode with ill-concealed disgust,
I went out to his crate, and in it I found a tin plate and a
battered tin mug of colossal proportions. When I returned
to the hut bearing these, Chumley brightened considerably,   65
and even went so far as to praise me for my intelligence.

'Ooooooooo, umph!' he said, and then crossed his legs
and continued his inspection of the hut. I sat down opposite
him and produced a packet of cigarettes. As I was selecting
one a long black arm was stretched across the table, and   70
Chumley grunted in delight. Wondering what he would do,
I handed him a cigarette, and to my astonishment he put it
carefully in the corner of his mouth. I lit my smoke and
handed Chumley the matches thinking that this would fool
him. He opened the box, took out a match, struck it, lit his   75
cigarette, threw the matches down on the table, crossed his
legs again and lay back in his chair inhaling thankfully and
blowing clouds of smoke out of his nose. Obviously he
had vices in his make-up of which I had been kept in
ignorance.   80

Just at that moment Pious entered bearing the tray of tea;
the effect on him when he saw me sitting at the table with

the chimp, smoking and apparently exchanging gossip, was considerable.

'Eh . . . eahh!' he gasped, backing away. 85

'Whar-hoooo,' said Chumley, sighting the tea and waving one hand madly.

'Na whatee that, sah?' asked Pious, from the doorway.

'This is Chumley,' I explained, 'he won't hurt you. Put the tea on the table.' 90

Pious did as he was told and then retreated to the door again. As I poured tea and milk into Chumley's mug, and added three tablespoons of sugar, he watched me with a glittering eye, and made a soft 'ooing' noise to himself. I handed him the mug and he took it carefully in both hands. 95 There was a moment's confusion when he tried to rid himself of the cigarette, which he found he could not hold as well as the mug; he solved the problem by placing the cigarette on the table. Then he tested the tea carefully with one lip stuck out, to see if it was too hot. As it was, he sat there and 100 blew on it until it was the right temperature, and then he drank it down. When he had finished the liquid there still remained the residue of syrupy sugar at the bottom. He balanced the mug on his nose and kept it there until the last of the sugar had trickled down into his mouth. Then he 105 held it out for a refill.

Objective Questions

1 'Visualised' (l. 10) means

    A planned to deal with
    B caught a glimpse of
    C had a mental picture of
    D dreamed of
    E expected to see

2 What surprised Durrell to begin with was Chumley's

    A size
    B calmness
    C similarity to a boxer
    D intelligence
    E age

3   'Sedately' (l. 13) means with

   A dignity
   B disappointment
   C solemnity
   D cheerlessness
   E composure

4   A word that is used in a colloquial sense is

   A 'star' (l. 16)
   B 'standing' (l. 16)
   C 'hairy' (l. 21)
   D 'terrific' (l. 34)
   E 'hit' (l. 34)

5   'Pugilistic' (l. 23) means like

   A an invalid
   B a gorilla
   C a mayor
   D a man with toothache
   E a boxer

6   By using the word 'glitter' (l. 36) Durrell suggests that Chumley's eyes revealed

   A sharp insight
   B concealed malice
   C stern resolution
   D mature disillusion
   E physical brightness

7   The essential point about Chumley is that he was so

   A surprising
   B self-confident
   C human
   D sophisticated
   E demanding

8   All the following phrases stress Chumley's self-confidence EXCEPT

   A stepped out (l. 15)
   B that made one feel uncomfortable (l. 37)

C with that bored expression that one sees on the
faces of professional hand-shakers (ll. 41–2)

D with the superb air of a Lord Mayor (l. 47)

E to walk into the hut as if he owned it (l. 51)

9 The following phrases make Chumley appear super-
cilious or contemptuous of mankind EXCEPT

A surveying our humble abode with ill-concealed
disgust (l. 62)

B went so far as to praise me (l. 66)

C he held it out for a refill (l. 106)

D smoking and apparently exchanging gossip (l. 83)

E Chumley wore the chain with the superb air of a
Lord Mayor (ll. 46–7)

10 Of the following definitions choose the MOST
INACCURATE:

A persisted in = continued (l. 28)

B ironic = meaning the opposite of what it *appears* to
mean (l. 36)

C shrewd = bad-tempered (l. 39)

D superb = impressive (l. 47)

E colossal = huge (l. 64)

11 Which ONE of the following remarks about punctuation
is NOT correct?

A In l. 2 the semi-colon is used to join two statements
both about Chumley.

B In l. 10 the colon is used to introduce a second
statement that repeats and emphasises the first
part of the sentence

C In l. 13 the purpose of the comma is to show that
seated does not describe the *van*

D In l. 23 the hyphen shows that the two halves of
the idea in *deep-set* have united to form one idea

E In l. 49 *which measured some fifteen feet* has two
commas because it is a defining clause, defining the
sort of chain that Chumley had.

12   Gerald Durrell suggests to us that when Pious first saw
      Chumley he was a little

    A excited
    B afraid
    C amused
    D angry
    E puzzled

2 Read the following article on Selborne Revisited and then
answer the questions that follow it.

Section A

    Gilbert White was born on July 18, 1720, in the parish of
Selborne in Hampshire, whose natural history he lived to
study for over 50 years. He was observing the countryside
during a long period of calm before the great agricultural
revolutions, which began with the enclosures and have   5
continued with increasing momentum ever since. Watching
over an unchanging scene he could gather his facts slowly,
assimilating the rhythm of the year. The letters which
comprise *The Natural History of Selborne* are the distillation of
a lifetime of rich and detailed experience.   10
    The natural historian of an English parish today cannot
expect to have such time for reflection. At least in the
intensively farmed areas of southern England, the amount of
change has probably been greater in the past 25 years than in
the preceding 250, and the consequence has been a continuous 15
erosion of the habitats of native plants and animals. Natural
deciduous woodland rich in species has given way to a
monoculture of barley or spruce. Hawthorn hedges where
wild birds nest and sing have been uprooted so that only
10 per cent remain. Meadows of daisies and buttercups have   20
been 'improved', yielding only rye-grass and cultivated strains
of 'wild' white clover. Verges, which are nature's highways
beside our own, have been sprayed with herbicides and
eroded by road widening on one side and ploughing on the
other. Ponds, over which dragonflies hawked and small boys   25
hung, first became rubbish dumps and then were filled in.
The meandering stream has become a mini-canal to accom-

modate the flash floods from the overdrained fields, and all
trees within 30 yards of the bank have been cut down to give
access to the dragline which removes at five-year intervals   30
any offensive plants which succeed in establishing themselves.

Although not all these changes have yet occurred in
every English parish, the warning signs are there, and for
the naturalist today it is these unnatural changes to which he
must give his greatest attention. There is no time to sit and   35
reflect for a lifetime, for if he fails to act now there will be
little wildlife to observe 50 years hence. The Gilbert White
days of the quiet naturalist have gone. Every parish needs
someone prepared to stand up and declare that wildlife can
no longer be taken for granted, to declare that the village   40
pond, the ridge-and-furrow meadow, the old chalk pit are
just as much a part of our heritage as the tithe barn or the
parish church. In parish and local council meetings the place
of wildlife conservation in the countryside must be
proclaimed.   45

But if the pleas are to be heard they must be backed by
facts. It is up to local naturalists to make a thorough survey
of their parish so that they know all the most important
areas for wildlife. It was with this in mind that the Cambridge-
shire and Isle of Ely Naturalists' Trust began in 1969 to   50
organise the writing of parish natural histories. Members of
the trust, the Women's Institutes, the primary schools and
village colleges have worked together in over 30 parishes to
prepare maps and lists, partly in order to discover areas
suitable for small nature reserves. They have produced   55
land utilization maps showing the major wildlife habitats:
woods, orchards, pastures, hedges and verges. They have
looked at the hedges with particular care to find those which
are richest in plant species: these are usually the oldest
hedges marking farm or parish boundaries.   60

Where the talent was available they have written a flora or
fauna of the parish. Children have prepared lists of birds,
mammals and butterflies which occur in their gardens: this
not only involved them in making observations, but their
combined results give an approximate idea of the compara-   65
tive abundance of different species at the present day. This is
very simple to collect and record, but it is surprising how little

of this kind of information is available from the past. For
instance, children could usefully record, like Gilbert White,
types of fish which anglers ignore but which he saw in streams.   70

Section B

We cannot stop the agricultural revolution. Destruction of
the countryside as we know it is bound to continue. We
must therefore think of every parish as the site of an emer-
gency archaeological natural history 'dig'. If a hedge can be
dated by its botanical composition (and the age of hedges   5
throws important light on the history of the village landscape) then if it is destroyed we may lose not only the
species in a hedge but an irreplaceable key to local history.
However, if the survey is a success and the pride and
understanding of local landowners and tenants can be   10
roused, the richest hedges will not be lost. It is hoped that
other similar areas—a green lane, an old moat or a parish pit
—will be taken over and managed by the people of the
parish for the people of the parish.

While some places may be saved merely as pleasant   15
features of village life, this is not enough: something must
also be done to replace the loss of wildlife habitats. Much of
the landscape as we knew it before 1945 was man-made:
the parkland of the estates, and the straight hawthorn hedges
of the enclosure fields, were planted in the seventeenth and   20
eighteenth centuries. If they are disappearing now, it is up to
this generation to ensure that they are replaced in a re-
designed landscape adapted to modern agriculture for the
benefit of our heirs in the twenty-first century.

Corners of land must be found in every parish for the   25
planting of trees. So much ugliness has been exposed in
the countryside by the clearing of hedges that most villages
would benefit visually from a wall of trees to break up their
stark outlines. But here again the voice of the naturalist
needs to be heard. Too often exotic trees are planted which 30
have few species of insect living on them, whereas native
species like the oak may play host to 150.

Exotic plants are of course expected and accepted in the
garden: but even here wise choice of flowers can help to

increase the wildlife of the parish. Buddleia, aubretia, aster,   35
alyssum, honesty, lavender and red valerian are all highly
attractive to butterflies—a group which is particularly
vulnerable to loss of suitable habitats in the surrounding
countryside. But they lay their eggs on native species which
must also be present to provide food for the larvae. Resisting   40
the temptation to slash ruthlessly at the nettle bed can
conserve wildlife and energy simultaneously. But above all
a garden can become a bird sanctuary. By feeding birds,
by creating scrub and woodland margin conditions which
suit most of our nesting birds because they are natives of   45
woodland, and by providing nestboxes for hole-nesting
species, we can begin to replace the losses of woodland and
hedgerow on the farm. If everyone plays his part we can look
forward to a landscape in which every village nestles in a
forest sheltering both birds and men.   50

Section A

1 The main reason why the natural historian today is not so
   fortunate as Gilbert White is that

    A the rate of change is much greater now
    B barley and spruce are grown more widely
    C the living places of some animals have disappeared
    D the system of enclosures spoilt the look of the
      countryside
    E Gilbert White had a long life in which to study

2 Which of the following are true about the days when
   Gilbert White lived?

    i they were in the eighteenth-century
    ii they followed the great agricultural revolutions
    iii the countryside was changing very slowly
    iv the naturalist had many others working in collabor-
      ation with him
    v naturalists had plenty of time for reflection
    A i, iii, and v
    B i, ii, and iv
    C ii, iii, and v
    D i, iv, and v
    E ii, iii, and iv

3 Which ONE of the following does this article NOT put
   forward as a reason for admiring Gilbert White's writing
   about Nature?

   A he gathered his facts with sensible slowness
   B he could ponder for fifty years on the wildlife of
      his parish
   C he observed nature in considerable detail
   D he was able to study the agricultural revolution as
      it happened
   E he kept his work in time with the changes of the
      seasons

4 'Eroded' (l. 24) means

   A worn away
   B destroyed gradually
   C reduced in size
   D spoilt
   E impaired

5 The section from l. 13 to l. 45 gives all the following
   reasons why the natural historian must act quickly
   today EXCEPT that

   A the countryside is changing far more rapidly than
      before
   B many native plants and animals have lost their
      homes
   C today a rural area contains fewer different types of
      plant
   D village ponds, which formerly attracted insects,
      have been filled in
   E too many fields are not properly drained and
      remain swamps

6 'Meandering' (l. 27) means

   A picturesque
   B rushing
   C winding
   D shallow
   E natural

D

7 The writer mentions that all the following parts of the village are worth preserving with the ONE EXCEPTION of the

    A village pond
    B tithe barn
    C parish church
    D village green
    E old chalk pit

8 By saying that 'the warning signs are there' (l. 33), the writer means that

    A speed-limit signs spoil the look of country lanes
    B the present state of the countryside is a warning for the future
    C the government should warn people against spoiling the countryside
    D in fifty years from now there will be no countryside left
    E it is in certain parts of the country that most harm has been done

9 Which ONE of the following is NOT among the activities of the Naturalists' Trust?

    A writing natural histories of parishes
    B choosing sites for possible nature reserves
    C producing land utilisation maps
    D studying hedges with great care
    E persuading local farmers to grow new crops

10 This section stresses that all the following are major homes for wildlife with the ONE EXCEPTION of

    A woods
    B orchards
    C ploughed fields
    D pasture land
    E grass verges

11 At different points in this article, but especially between
    ll. 13–31 and ll. 58–60, the writer emphasises that the
    destruction of hedges will have all the following results
    EXCEPT
        A there will be fewer places for birds to nest
        B we shall lose the traditional method of dividing
           fields
        C we shall lose all the plants growing in or near the
           hedges
        D farmers will benefit from having fewer hedges to
           keep tidy
        E we shall lose a valuable guide to the history of the
           parish

12 This article urges the local naturalist to collect all the
    following information EXCEPT
        A facts about the areas that are most helpful and
           hospitable to wildlife
        B facts about the areas that could most convincingly
           be turned into small nature reserves
        C maps that show woods, orchards, pastures, hedges
           and road verges
        D the position of the hedges that shelter the widest
           variety of plants
        E geological facts about the make-up of the soils in
           different gardens

13 Which ONE of the following have children NOT done
        A studied the living places of wild animals and birds
        B recorded the names of birds and butterflies seen
           in their gardens
        C identified the kinds of fish in their streams
        D made a special study of hedges
        E collected rare plants from hedges

Section B

14 The phrase' an irreplaceable key to local history' (l. 8) means that students of the past of a particular parish are provided with

    A a memorial of the past
    B a solution to problems concerned with the past
    C an illustration of the past
    D the site where the development of the past began
    E a commentary on the technical problems of the past

15 'Richest hedges' (l. 11) are those which

    A tell us most about the past
    B contain the widest variety of plants
    C both tell us most about the past and contain the widest variety of plants
    D contain trees and plants with a commercial value
    E possess the most luxuriant growth

16 As used in l. 30 and l. 33 'exotic' means

    A made of plastic
    B strange and unusual
    C bizarre and luxuriant
    D having comparatively few leaves
    E introduced from abroad

17 'Simultaneously' (l. 42) means

    A quickly
    B slowly
    C at the same time
    D in a hurry
    E irrevocably

18 The one of the following words that is used metaphorically (i.e. figuratively) is

    A 'visually' (l. 28)
    B 'species' (l. 31)
    C 'host' (l. 32)
    D 'wise' (l. 34)
    E 'attractive' (l. 37)

19 By which of the following can a garden do a lot to
conserve threatened species?

     i providing a bird sanctuary
    ii growing plants attractive to butterflies
   iii removing untidy plants such as nettles
   iv providing nesting-boxes for birds
    v providing suitable places for birds to feed in winter

    A i, ii, iii, and iv
    B i, ii, iv, and v
    C i, ii, iii, and v
    D ii, iii, iv, and v
    E all of them

Other Questions

1 Explain briefly why Dr Perring, the author of this article,
admires Gilbert White

2 Explain why it is necessary for the natural historian of today
to act quickly

3 Analyse and classify the types of information that the local
naturalist must collect (with or without helpers) in order to
plead his case more convincingly

4 What sorts of information must be collected quickly
before they are destroyed for ever?

5 What steps can be taken to preserve wild life in every parish?

TEST 8

A Write a composition on one of these topics:

    1 Describe the scene, the setting and the mood of the spectators *before* an important sporting event, and then describe the first moments of the event. You may break off in the middle as though the rest of the event will be described on a later sheet of paper temporarily missing

    2 A short story beginning, 'After a moment's hesitation, I opened the door and went in'

    3 'Some rooms seem to have a personality of their own, to be warm and friendly or cold and off-putting. This may be as true of new rooms as of old rooms.' Describe one or more rooms that have had this effect on you

    4 A visit to a well-known seaside resort in winter

    5 A scene at a busy seaport or airport

    6 'The best things in life are free'

B Write about 250 words on One of the following:

    1 Imagine you are the secretary of a local Youth Club and are sending some necessary information to a visiting speaker. Among the points you wish to mention are the following:

        The location of your club and the best ways of reaching it by car and by public transport.

        The age-range of those who usually attend, the relative proportions of boys and girls, the average attendance at meeting.

        The subject on which you are inviting him (or her) to speak, with some guidance as to how long he should speak and whether questions and discussion usually follow the talk.

        Arrangements to meet him when he arrives and for entertaining him after the talk.

        Your gratitude to him for agreeing to come to speak to your club.

    You may include as many of the above points as you wish

and add any others which you think would be relevant and helpful.

2 Here is a description in note form of the Mole. Write it as a continuous piece of English:

Mole. Lives underground. Pushes up earth from excavated tunnels causing molehills. Food mainly earthworms and some insect grubs. Body of soft velvety fur. Short neck. Eyes very small. Forelimbs like wide open hands. Used for tunnelling. Poor sense of sight. Highly developed sense of smell. Eyes have eyeballs with lenses. But virtually blind. Hunts by scent. Home of mole is underground chamber. About a foot high and three feet broad. Nest is ball of leaves or grass. Mating season end of March. Litter from two to seven. Has few enemies. Can swim excellently. Does not hibernate. Helps farmer and gardener by eating wireworms, leather-jackets, cockchafer grubs. Does good by helping drainage. Moles which tunnel under tennis lawns or golf greens must be killed. Plentiful in all parts of the British Isles where earthworms are found.
(You may change the order of the facts given, omit some and if you wish add to them.)

C Write one of the letters below:

1 You have bought some article through the post and find that it is not up to the standard you had been led to expect. Write a suitable letter to the firm which supplied it
2 Suggest to the local public librarian the titles of several books you think would interest many readers of your age-group. Give reasons for your choice

Section II SUMMARY AND COMPREHENSION

1 Read the following passage and then answer the questions on it:

My birthday was due fairly soon, and if I dealt with the family skilfully I felt sure that I could get not only a boat, but a lot of other equipment as well. I therefore suggested to the family that, instead of letting them choose my birthday

presents, I might tell them the things I wanted most. In this   5
way they could be sure of not disappointing me. The
family, rather taken aback, agreed, and then, somewhat
suspiciously, asked me what I wanted. Innocently, I said
that I hadn't thought about it much, but that I would work
out a list for each person, and they could then choose one or   10
more items on it.

My list took a lot of time and thought to work out, and a
considerable amount of applied psychology. Mother, for
instance, I knew, would buy me everything on her list, so I
put down the most necessary and expensive equipment: 15
five wooden cases, glass-topped, cork-lined, to house my
insect collection; two dozen test tubes; five pints of
methylated spirits, five pints of formalin, and a microscope.
Margo's list was a little more difficult, for the items had to be
chosen so that they would encourage her to go to her   20
favourite shop. So from her I asked for ten yards of butter
muslin, ten yards of white calico, six large packets of pins,
two bundles of cotton wool, two pints of ether, a pair of
forceps, and two fountain-pen fillers. It was, I realised
resignedly, quite useless to ask Larry for anything like   25
formalin or pins, but if my list showed some sort of literary
leaning I stood a good chance. Accordingly I made out a
formidable sheet covered with the titles, authors' names,
publishers, and price of all the natural history books I felt in
need of, and put an asterisk against those that would be   30
most gratefully received. Since I had only one request left,
I decided to tackle Leslie verbally instead of handing him a
list, but I knew I should have to choose my moment with
care. I had to wait some days for what I considered to be a
propitious moment.   35

I had just helped him to the successful conclusion of some
ballistic experiments he was making, which involved tying
an ancient muzzle-loader to a tree and firing it by means of
a long string attached to the trigger. At the fourth attempt
we achieved what apparently Leslie considered to be a   40
success: the barrel burst and bits of metal whined in all
directions. Leslie was delighted and made copious notes on
the back of an envelope. Together we set about picking up the
remains of the gun. While we were thus engaged I casually

asked what he would like to give me for my birthday.   45

'Hadn't thought about it,' he replied absently, examining
with evident satisfaction a contorted piece of metal. 'I don't
mind . . . anything you like . . . you choose.'

I said I wanted a boat. Leslie, realising how he had been
trapped, said indignantly that a boat was far too large a   50
present for a birthday, and anyway he couldn't afford it.
I said, equally indignantly, that he had *told* me to choose what
I liked. Leslie said yes, he had, but he hadn't meant a boat,
as they were terribly expensive. I said that when one said
anything one meant anything, which included boats, and anyway   55
I didn't expect him to buy me one. I had thought, since he
knew so much about boats, he would be able to build me
one. However, if he thought that would be too difficult . . .

'Of course it's not difficult,' said Leslie, unguardedly, and
then added hastily, 'Well . . . not terribly difficult. But it's the   60
time. It would take ages and ages to do. Look, wouldn't it
be better if I took you out in the *Sea Cow* twice a week?'

But I was adamant; I wanted a boat and I was quite prepared to wait for it.

'Oh, all right, all right,' said Leslie exasperatedly, 'I'll build   65
you a boat, but I'm not having you hanging around while
I do it, understand? You're to keep well away. You're not to
see it until it's finished.'

(In two weeks' time the boat was finished and his birthday arrived.)

My presents having been duly inspected and the family   70
thanked, I then went round to the back veranda with Leslie,
and there lay a mysterious shape covered with a tarpaulin.
Leslie drew this aside with the air of a conjuror, and there
lay my boat. I gazed at it rapturously; it was surely the
most perfect boat that anyone had ever had. Gleaming in   75
her coat of new paint she lay there, my steed to the enchanted
archipelago.

The boat was some seven feet long, and almost circular in
shape. Leslie explained hurriedly—in case I thought the
shape was due to defective workmanship—that the reason for   80
this was that the planks had been too short for the frame,
an explanation I found perfectly satisfactory. After all, it
was the sort of irritating thing that could have happened to
anyone. I said stoutly that I thought it was a lovely shape for

a boat, and indeed I thought it was. She was not sleek, slim, 85
and rather predatory looking, like most boats, but rotund,
placid, and somehow comforting in her circular solidarity.
She reminded me of an earnest dungbeetle, an insect for
which I had great affection. Leslie, pleased at my evident
delight, said deprecatingly that he had been forced to make 90
her flat-bottomed, since, for a variety of technical reasons,
this was the safest. I said that I liked flat-bottomed boats the
best, because it was possible to put jars of specimens on the
floor without so much risk of them upsetting. Leslie asked me
if I liked the colour scheme, as he had not been too sure about 95
it. Now, in my opinion, the colour scheme was the best
thing about it, the final touch that completed the unique
craft. Inside she was painted green and white, while her
bulging sides were tastefully covered in white, black, and
brilliant orange stripes, a combination of colours that 100
struck me as being both artistic and friendly. Leslie then
showed me the long, smooth cypress pole he had cut for a
mast, but explained that it could not be fitted into position
until the boat was launched. Enthusiastically I suggested
launching her at once. Leslie, who was a stickler for 105
procedure, said you couldn't launch a ship without naming
her, and had I thought of a name yet? This was a difficult
problem, and the whole family were called out to help me
solve it. They stood clustered round the boat, which looked
like a gigantic flower in their midst, and racked their brains. 110

'Why not call it the *Jolly Roger*?' suggested Margo.

I rejected this scornfully; I explained that I wanted a sort
of fat name that would go with the boat's appearance and
personality.

'*Arbuckle*?' suggested Mother vaguely. 115

That was no use either; the boat simply didn't look like
an Arbuckle.

'Call it the *Ark*,' said Leslie, but I shook my head.

There was another silence, while we all stared at the boat.
Suddenly I had it, the perfect name: *Bootle*, that's what I'd 120
call her.

'Very nice, dear,' approved Mother.

'I was just going to suggest the *Bumtrinket*,' said Larry.

After much thought I decided what to do. A pot of black

paint was produced and laboriously, in rather trickly capitals,   125
I traced her name along the side: *The Bootle-Bumtrinket.*

(a) Comment on the effectiveness of the words 'suspiciously' (l. 8), and 'innocently' (l. 8)

(b) His list needed 'a considerable amount of applied
psychology' he says. By reference to the rest of the
paragraph, but without giving details, explain what
he meant by this

(c) At the end of the second paragraph, he says he had to
wait 'for a propitious moment'. Explain this, and in a
sentence give the circumstances in which the moment
arrived

(d) Comment on the effectiveness of his remark 'However,
if he thought that would be too difficult . . .' (l. 58)

(e) Quote the sentence in ll. 78–110 which shows that
the writer thought the shape of the boat better than
that of normal boats. Would most people have agreed
with him?

(f) Two features of the boat, other than its shape, might
have been considered unusual. What were these,
and how did Gerald Durrell show his brother that
these features pleased him?

(g) Leslie was 'a stickler for procedure' (l. 105). What
does this mean in the passage?

(h) Explain each of the following:
some sort of literary leaning (l. 26)
tackle Leslie verbally (l. 32)
with evident satisfaction (l. 47)
realising how he had been trapped (l. 49)
I was adamant (l. 63)

(i) What do you learn of Gerald Durrell as a boy from
this extract from his book about his life on the island
of Corfu?

(j) Use your own words to show that you understand the
meanings that these italicised phrases have in their
context:
i the family, *rather taken aback* (l. 7)
ii Margo's list was *a little more difficult* (l. 19)

(k) Suppose that you are Leslie and you keep a diary.
What would you write in it about
    i your experiments with ballistics
    ii your building of Gerald's boat and your feelings
      towards Gerald?

Objective Questions

Answer each of the following questions by writing down the
letter that stands for the best answer.

1 'Dealt with' (l. 1) suggests that Gerald

    A flattered his family
    B appealed to his family
    C bargained with his family
    D controlled his family
    E handled his family skilfully

2 When Gerald first asked the family to let him choose
his birthday presents they were

    A caught unawares
    B embarrassed
    C surprised
    D outmanoeuvred
    E put off their guard

3 A word in the first two paragraphs that is used ironically
(to mean the opposite of what it really means) is

    A 'skilfully' (l. 2)
    B 'innocently' (l. 8)
    C 'suspiciously' (l. 8)
    D 'difficult' (l. 19)
    E 'gratefully' (l. 31)

4 That the writer, Gerald Durrell, was later to become a
collector of animals is evident from

    A especially the presents he sought from his mother
    B all the presents that he asked for
    C his requests to his mother and Mary
    D his skill in manipulating his family
    E his passion for flat-bottomed boats

TEST 11 (Derelict Land)		TEST 11 (Hitler)		TEST 12 (Antigone)		TEST 13 (Women in Business)		TEST 14 (The Press)	
1	E	1	D	1	A	1	B	1	D
2	A	2	D	2	E	2	B	2	B
3	D	3	E	3	E	3	E	3	D
4	C	4	C	4	E	4	C	4	A
5	B	5	C	5	B	5	E	5	B
6	D	6	D	6	D	6	D	6	C
7	E	7	A	7	B	7	B	7	C
8	B	8	C	8	A	8	D	8	C
9	E	9	D	9	D	9	A	9	C
10	B	10	E	10	C	10	A	10	A
11	D	11	A	11	E	11	B	11	D
12	C	12	E	12	B	12	A	12	A
13	A	13	C	13	D	13	A	13	B
14	C	14	D	14	C	14	D	14	C
15	B	15	D	15	C	15	E	15	B
16	C	16	B			16	B	16	D
17	C	17	C			17	A	17	A
18	C	18	C	TEST 12 (Bondi)		18	C	18	B
19	B	19	D			19	E	19	D
20	E	20	B			20	D	20	D
21	A			1	E	21	B	21	B
22	C			2	B	22	D	22	C
23	C			3	C	23	C		
24	A			4	D				
25	C			5	B				
26	A			6	B				
				7	C				
				8	B				
				9	D				
				10	B				
				11	C				
				12	C				
				13	E				
				14	A				
				15	A				
				16	E				

TEST 8 (Water-ways)		TEST 9 (Treasure-hunting)		TEST 9 (Roman Chester)		TEST 10 (Insects)		TEST 10 (Words-worth)	
1	B	1	B	1	C	1	D	1	B
2	A	2	A	2	D	2	D	2	B
3	D	3	B	3	C	3	A	3	A
4	D	4	D	4	E	4	C	4	C
5	B	5	C	5	A	5	B	5	B
6	D	6	D	6	E	6	C	6	D
7	D	7	A	7	B	7	B	7	A
8	D	8	E	8	C	8	D	8	D
9	E	9	A	9	A	9	B	9	B
10	E	10	D	10	C	10	A	10	A
11	E	11	C	11	A	11	A	11	E
12	D	12	A	12	E	12	E	12	D
13	A	13	C	13	E	13	D	13	A
14	A	14	A	14	B	14	D	14	A
15	C	15	B	15	C	15	B	15	B
16	C	16	C	16	B	16	C	16	E
17	B	17	C	17	D	17	C	17	D
18	E	18	A	18	A	18	C	18	E
19	A	19	A	19	D	19	A	19	D
20	D	20	C	20	E	20	E	20	E
21	B							21	A
								22	B

Answers to Objective Questions

TEST 6 (Death of Gordon)		TEST 6 (Old England)		TEST 7 (Cholmond-eley)		TEST 7 (Gilbert White)		TEST 8 (Durrell)	
1	B	1	E	1	C	1	A	1	E
2	E	2	B	2	A	2	A	2	C
3	D	3	A	3	E	3	D	3	B
4	B	4	C	4	D	4	C	4	B
5	B	5	C	5	E	5	E	5	A
6	D	6	B	6	A	6	C	6	C
7	A	7	D	7	C	7	D	7	B
8	A	8	D	8	A	8	B	8	D
9	C	9	D	9	C	9	E	9	B
10	E	10	C	10	C	10	C	10	C
11	C	11	E	11	E	11	D	11	B
12	A	12	B	12	B	12	E	12	B
13	E	13	E			13	E	13	D
14	C	14	B			14	B	14	C
15	C	15	E			15	C	15	A
16	D	16	B			16	E	16	A
17	A	17	D			17	C	17	D
18	B	18	C			18	C	18	B
19	B	19	C			19	B	19	B
20	A	20	A					20	C
		21	C					21	D
								22	B
								23	E

5 Which of the following comments on metaphors is NOT
   true?

   A in l. 8 the family's reaction to the narrator's
      request is compared to a policeman's reaction to
      the presence of a thief
   B in l. 32 the narrator's approach to Leslie is
      compared to that of a defender in a game trying
      to dispossess an attacker
   C in l. 41 the noise made by bits of metal is compared
      to the high-pitched complaining of a man or
      animal
   D In l. 76 the boat that will transport him out to sea
      is compared to a magic horse on which he could
      fly to an enchanted island
   E in l. 109 the family standing round the boat is com-
      pared to a number of fruits or flowers growing
      together

6 Gerald showed his 'considerable amount of applied
   psychology' in the following ways:–

     i he asked his generous mother to give him most
    ii he counted on his sister wanting to visit one type of
        shop
   iii he exploited Larry's interest in books
    iv he chose Leslie's moment of triumph to ask for a
        boat
     v he wanted to give his boat a romantic name
         A i, ii and iii
         B i, ii and iv
         C i, ii, iii and iv
         D i, iii and v
         E all of them.

7 'Resignedly' (l. 25) means
     A with an obvious inability to understand his brother
     B accepting the inevitable without a big effort
     C coolly and philosophically
     D accepting a partial defeat without regret
     E with a gloomy air of disappointment

8 Which of the following could NOT be deduced from Gerald's tactics?

    A his mother was comparatively rich
    B Margo was more likely to go to one shop than to another
    C his brother, Larry, showed when young the interest in books that later led him to write novels
    D his brother, Leslie, was more interested in scientific theories than in putting them into practice
    E the personalities and interests of the family were strikingly different

9 'Propitious' (l. 35) means

    A lucky
    B favourable
    C effective
    D timely
    E persuasive

10 'Ballistic experiments' (l. 37) concern

    A guns
    B science
    C missiles
    D mock-warfare
    E chemistry

11 The use of the word 'casually' (l. 44) is

    A an unintentional exaggeration
    B an amusing reversal of the truth
    C an example of the author's occasional mistake
    D a confession of the author's deliberate deception
    E a half-hearted attempt at an excuse

12 Leslie was 'trapped' (l. 50) in that he was persuaded to give Gerald a boat when he was

    A thinking of other things at the time
    B preoccupied and thrilled with his success
    C tempted to be glib
    D asked to do what he was good at
    E beaten in argument and outwitted by Gerald

13 'I was adamant' (l. 63) meant that Gerald

    A still hoped to get his boat
    B prepared to wait patiently
    C greedily demanded all he wanted
    D stubbornly refused to change his mind
    E skilfully resisted his brother's arguments

14 When Gerald first saw the boat he stared at it with

    A mild surprise
    B moderate delight
    C great enthusiasm
    D expert appreciation
    E pretended gratitude

15 Gerald's attitude to the boat is not clearly explained; but
    presumably he

    A was more thrilled with it than his brother had
       expected
    B pretended not to see its faults
    C judged it only by its suitability for swimming
       excursions
    D disliked the colours of the paint
    E had always wanted a round flat-bottomed boat

16 Gerald, writing as an adult, suggests a contrast between
    his attitude to the boat when looking back on it as an
    adult, and the thrill he felt about it at the time. He
    suggests this contrast in the last paragraphs by

    A expressing his childhood delight in exaggerated
       terms
    B comparing a sluggish, round boat to a magic
       'steed'
    C giving over-emphasis to Leslie's apologies for its
       faults
    D comparing the boat to a dung-beetle, an un-
       attractive insect
    E insisting that Leslie was a stickler for procedure

17 'Predatory' (l. 86) normally describes animals or people who

    A look contented like a cow
    B are concerned with their own selfish interests
    C repeatedly feel hungry
    D live by preying on others
    E are used for not quite respectable purposes

18 The following words are applied to aspects of the boat by Gerald as terms of almost meaningless praise with the ONE EXCEPTION of

    A 'lovely' (l. 84)
    B 'bulging' (l. 99)
    C 'tastefully' (l. 99)
    D 'artistic' (l. 101)
    E 'friendly' (l. 101)

19 That Leslie was a 'stickler for procedure' (l. 105) means that he

    A wanted to proceed immediately
    B insisted on things being done correctly
    C thought that he knew better than others
    D was an expert in launching a boat
    E delighted in delaying the launching

20 Which of these facts about Leslie become apparent?

    i he had serious limitations as a carpenter
    ii when doing a job, he became completely absorbed in it
    iii he sometimes spoke hastily before thinking carefully
    iv he was Gerald Durrell's favourite brother
    v he thought no boat should be launched un-named

        A i, ii and iii
        B ii, iii and iv
        C i, ii, iii and v
        D i, iv and v
        E ii, iii and v

21 'Evident' (l. 89) means

    A grateful
    B immediate
    C detectable
    D obvious
    E sincere

22 The boat looked like a gigantic 'flower' because of its

    A usefulness
    B bright colours
    C unusual shape
    D flat bottom
    E safety factor

23 Which ONE of the following remarks about the choice of
names is NOT correct?

    A Margo thought of the boat as belonging to a
pirate
    B Mrs Durrell compared it to a comedian well
known for his fatness
    C Leslie thought of it as a boat likely to be used for
transporting animals—or at least insects
    D Gerald wanted a romantic name
    E Larry tried to choose a name that would include
everyone else's ideas

2
Section A

In the remote dawn of history our ancestors were nomads.
When the days lengthened they would leave their sheltered
winter camping-grounds in the river valleys and move with
their flocks and herds to the sweeter airs and fresh herbage of
the upland pastures, leaving little behind them but the cool-   5
ing ashes of their camp fires. Centuries of settled civilisation
now divide us from these ancestors, and yet there must be
few who do not at times feel a restlessness which is no less
than the old nomadic instinct astir within us. It is the same
instinct which invests such simple words as 'over the hills   10
and far away' with the magic of an incantation.

It is for this reason, I believe, that of all the ingenious
inventions which man has perfected those connected with

transport appeal most strongly to our imagination, and none
more strongly than ships and railways. It may be that no   15
work of man's hands can ever equal or surpass the grandeur
of the tall sailing ship; but the fact remains that any ship,
whether she be a great liner, a dirty little coaster or a fishing
boat, fascinates us because she is imbued with the mystery
and magic of the sea—the lure of those far horizons which   20
lie beyond the flashing of the harbour lights. This magic is no
romantic illusion of the landsman. The sea changes a man's
nature unmistakably and binds him to her in such a way
that no matter how he may complain of the hardships she
imposes, the seaman can seldom bring himself to leave her.   25

Section B

It is more difficult to analyse the magic of the railways, but
for all that it is no less real. There is no air of mystery about the
steam locomotive, for she travels a steel road, man-made and
circumscribed. When the small coaster slips down the estuary
with the evening tide and we watch her till she is no more   5
than a smudge of smoke against the sunset on the horizon's
rim it is easy to believe her to be bound for the Hesperides.
But we can harbour no such illusion as we stand on the platform of a London terminus and watch the departure of a
northbound express. Her destination is certain, yet the   10
fascination is there, and is even due to the fact that in addition
to the romance of her swift far journey, our imagination is
captured by the magnitude of the engineering works and the
complexity of the organisation which makes that certainty
possible. The winking tail lamps fade away over the   15
gleaming mesh of rails; we can no longer hear the heavy
exhaust beats; signal lights flick from green to red or amber.
But still the mind's eye can follow the progress of the
express as she gathers speed. We can imagine her thundering
over lofty viaducts or plunging with a scream into long   20
tunnels as she races northwards, the glare from her open
firedoor lighting up the flying steam. And always the
signal lights herald her coming and guard her passing as the
signalmen in their lonely boxes flash their message northwards and peg their block instruments to 'Train on Line'.   25

Yes, the appeal of the railway is a composite one, not dependent wholly upon the locomotive, but compounded of everything that makes the railway system. It has captivated generations of laymen, while the railwayman, like the seaman, acquires a certain indefinable character and tradition.   30
He lives in a world of his own.

Section C

Another world, far less widely known but combining some features common both to the sea and to the railways, is that represented by the Inland Waterways of England. The navigable river is the road to the sea, while the canals which connect these rivers resemble the railways with their   5
important junctions, their main and branch lines, their tunnels and aqueducts. Yet however narrow, shallow and man-made these canals may be, they seem to bring into the very heart of England something of the sea's magic. For they are water roads, and so their traffic is not bounded, in   10
imagination at least, by those limitations which the tarmac or the steel rail impose. We may not appreciate this as we lean over the parapet of the old bridge at the foot of the village street and watch the ducks dabbling in the water or the small boys with net and jar fishing for stickleback. The canal   15
looks as domesticated as a village duck pond. It is only when we notice that the little pub by the bridge bears the sign of 'The Anchor', 'The Navigation', or 'The Lord Nelson' that we begin to realise that it represents a world beyond the small, ordered and centuries-old routine of village life;   20
that if we were to follow the waterway where it curves out of sight between the high hedges, it would lead us eventually to the river, and down the river to the sea. Perhaps a boat will pass by, shattering the smooth mirror of the water, setting the reeds swaying, frightening the ducks, and exciting   25
the small boys, but soon vanishing to leave everything as still and as tranquil as before. Her errand may be prosaic enough, did we but know it, but if we have any imagination we may experience again something of that sense of wonder and sur-mise with which we watched the coasting steamer sail into   30
the sunset.

Objective Questions

Section A

1 This writer's conception of nomads includes all the following ideas EXCEPT that they

   A rarely moved their animals to new grazing grounds

   B had already developed agriculture

   C had no settled home

   D belonged, it seems, always to the past

   E had different instincts from those of modern man

2 These two paragraphs are an appropriate way of beginning the preface to a book on canals because they

   A explain the thrill of everything connected with travel

   B are intended to provide an interesting contrast with what follows

   C emphasise the unrivalled impressiveness of sailing ships

   D stress the glamour of the sea, not the cosiness of canals

   E regard canals as part of the romantic scenery of Britain

3 Which one of the following did NOT occur when the nomads left the valleys?

   A summer had already arrived

   B there was no longer the need to be sheltered from winds

   C the air on the hills seemed cleaner and healthier

   D they set fire to their previous camping grounds

   E the grass in the valleys looked short and tired where their camps

4 'But' (l. 5) means

   A merely

   B just

   C only

   D except

   E whereas

5   The one idea that this section stresses most is that
     prehistoric nomads and modern men

     A are centuries apart from one another
     B share the same instinctive love of travel
     C are very different from one another
     D experience the same emotions in their social life
     E are both difficult to please and are at times
        discontented

6   An 'instinct' (l. 9) is

     A an unreasonable tendency to act in a certain way
     B an elaborate pattern of reaction to stimuli
     C an immediate reaction to a situation
     D an inherited tendency to act in a certain way
     E a romantic faith in the desirability of change

7   An 'incantation' (l. 11) is a

     A rhyme
     B motto
     C miracle
     D spell
     E lucky charm

8   'Imbued with' (l. 19) means

     A penetrated by
     B dyed with
     C inspired by
     D filled with
     E associated with

9   The main idea of the second paragraph is that

     A landsmen imagine sailors are thrilled by the sea
     B inventions that are ingenious have a special appeal
     C ships become more sophisticated machines
     D the true sailor can never leave a life at sea
     E all ships (and also railways) captivate most people

10 An 'illusion' (l. 22) is a

    A mistake
    B deception
    C misunderstanding
    D inaccurate impression
    E mistaken belief

Section B

11 As seen in Section B the railway engine is different from ships in all the following respects EXCEPT that

    A its charm is harder to understand
    B its appearance and actions are more lacking in mystery
    C its route is more definite
    D its destination is more likely to be known by onlookers
    E we are less likely to visualise its destination

12 This writer talks of the Hesperides (l. 7), who were nymphs guarding the golden apples, as though they were

    A gates to the kingdom of death
    B a land where the past was forgotten
    C a realm populated by fabulous monsters
    D islands where everyone was happy
    E a shadowy land inhabited by the ghosts of cowards

13 Section B looks at a train from the point of view of the

    A spectator
    B geographer
    C traveller
    D historian
    E engine-driver

14 'Circumscribed' (l. 4) means

    A restricted
    B well-known
    C straightened
    D localised
    E identified

15 Which of the following aspects of a railway journey
from London to the north are mentioned?
  i we know for certain where it will end
  ii the long journey is completed quickly
  iii a vast amount of engineering makes it possible
  iv intricate arrangements are needed for it
  v a train itself creates a beautiful scene
      A i, ii and iii
      B i, ii, iii and v
      C i, iii, iv and v
      D ii, iii, iv and v
      E all of them

16 Which one of the following points about the interest
and romance of railway travel is NOT mentioned by this
writer?
    A it is created by many things, besides the locomotive
      itself
    B it has appealed to people at different times in modern
      history
    C it has been diminished by the passing of the steam
      locomotive
    D it is made up of many different elements
    E it has led to the railway worker, like the seaman,
      acquiring a distinctive character

17 In the context of l. 29, 'laymen' describes men who are
NOT
    A priests
    B railwaymen
    C trainspotters
    D travellers
    E scholars

Section C

18 By which of the following facts is Section C linked to
the previous paragraph?

    i both make some mention of the sea

    ii the word 'world' (l. 31B and l. 1C) is repeated as
    a link-word

    iii railways and inland waterways are both compli-
    cated systems with junctions, etc.

    iv both railways and canals appeal to our romantic
    imagination

    v we are made to think about the remote destination
    of the railway and canal

        A i, iii and iv
        B i, iii, iv and v
        C i, ii, iii and iv
        D ii, iii, iv and v
        E all of them

19 The canal resembles the village duck-pond because it

    A looks an essential part of a homely English scene
    B represents a recent innovation
    C is more widely connected with the greater mari-
    time world
    D should appeal more strongly to our imagination
    and wonder
    E brings into the village names more closely
    connected with the sea

20 Which one of the following words is NOT used in a
metaphorical or figurative way but is used literally?

    A 'road' (l. 4)
    B 'heart' (l. 9)
    C 'magic' (l. 9)
    D 'routine' (l. 20)
    E 'mirror' (l. 24)

21   Prosaic' (l. 27) means
     A commercial
     B unromantic
     C unnoticed
     D uninteresting
     E traditional

Other questions

1 This passage is the first part of the preface to a book called
   The Inland Waterways of England. Discuss to what extent you
   think it appropriate to its purpose
2 Write 10–15 lines commenting on the variety of the writer's
   interests
3 Suggest two reasons why you can deduce that this book was
   written in 1947 rather than in the 1970's

CHAPTER EIGHT

Punctuation

When you were younger, someone probably told you to insert a mark of punctuation where you would pause for breath if you were reading aloud. This was not very good advice. It is roughly true of the more important stops, such as full-stops. But it is a poor guide to the insertion of commas, which in modern English have become much more a guide to silent understanding than to reading aloud.

About two-thirds of punctuation is a matter of rules, where the use of a certain stop can be right or wrong, but about one-third of punctuation is a matter of personal choice.

The following notes remind you of some of the main uses of certain stops.

Commas

1 Certain clauses are called defining clauses: e.g.
> The Melbourne *that is in Derbyshire* is far less famous than its Australian counterpart.

The clause in italics defines which Melbourne we are talking about, and is absolutely essential to the sense of the sentence. So it is not cut off from the rest of the sentence by commas as is the non-defining clause in the following sentence:
> Melbourne, *which is named after Queen Victoria's first Prime Minister*, is the second largest city in Victoria.

This clause is not essential to the sense, and we do not use it to define which Melbourne we are talking about; so we give the clause two commas. These commas divide it off from the rest of the sentence and show that it is a less imprtant idea, added as an aside.

2 Many sentences contain minor clauses or phrases: e.g.
> Six hundred engineers *stationed at Ripon* will spend next

month in the Highlands. There they will live in tents *wherever these can be pitched* and will build new amenities *such as roads and bridges* that the Highlands need badly. The three clauses or phrases in italics are something like the defining and non-defining clauses already discussed. But it is difficult to say dogmatically whether they are defining or non-defining. The only rule is that you must make up your mind; you must give each group of words two commas or none. The more you regard the groups of words as essential to the sense, the more likely you are to give them no commas.

3 *Punctuating a list:* When two nouns are joined by 'and', as in

A and B

fish and chips

there is no comma before 'and'.

When the list is longer, it is usual to join the last pair by 'and' without a comma and to join the others by a comma:

A, B, C, D and F

Blackpool, Fleetwood and Lancaster.

But where this custom leads to ambiguity, then it is necessary to precede the last 'and' by a comma:

Their favourite foods were steak, blackcurrant tart, fish and chips, and biscuits.

Similarly, it is not always necessary to put a comma before 'and' or 'but' when one of them introduces a group of words; but whenever 'and' or 'but' introduces an emphatically different idea, put a comma in front of it, e.g.

The boxer knocked down his opponent, and the referee stopped the fight.

(At a first glance this sentence would read oddly if we omitted the comma.)

4 *Dividing the Subject from the Verb:* You should not divide the verb from its subject or its object by a single comma. Indeed a pair of commas is less of a barrier than a single comma, because a pair of commas normally brackets off a phrase of minor importance. The single comma in the following sentence wrongly divides the main verb (*are*) from an essential part of the sentence:

Most accidents in the modern motor-car, are the result of fatigue on the part of the driver.

5 *A Comma instead of a heavier stop:* The worst error with a comma is to use it in between two sentences where a heavier stop is needed, as in this sentence:

A reporter is never off duty, he may be called upon at any time to travel anywhere.

Here a semi-colon is needed.

Semi-Colons

1 Consider the following example:

Do not be afraid of the semi-colon; it can be very useful. Each half of this could be a separate sentence, but to write the two halves separately would make your style too jerky. In this sort of instance a semi-colon is useful to tie together two statements on the same topic.

2 A semi-colon is valuable as a means of dividing up a sentence into sections when a comma is not strong enough because commas are already being used in the sentence for more trivial functions. J. B. Priestley provides an extreme example of this:

'I know and have a growing affection for the real America, the place itself where the real people live: for Central Park on a Sunday morning and the magical towers of New York at dusk; for those white villages among the flaring woods of New England in the fall; for the majestic rivers I have crossed so many times, the trains hooting so mournfully as night descends on the immense, sad plains; for the sparkle and sharp fragrance, the blue air and distant violet ranges of the desert; for the Pacific dimpling beyond the solemn groves of giant trees; and for all the people, or most of them, I have talked to, eaten and drunk with, cursed or kissed, across those three thousand miles.'

3 A semi-colon can be used to sharpen a contrast when the two halves of a sentence are similar in structure, but opposite in meaning:

'The western part of England has mild winters because of the ice-free Gulf Stream; the eastern part is exposed to bitterly cold east winds from snowbound Europe.'

4 A semi-colon is one way of avoiding the over-use of the word 'and'. Instead of writing—

He dug the garden for most of the morning, and planted
part of it, and then began to tire.
you can write—
He dug the garden for most of the morning and planted
part of it; then he began to tire.

The Colon

1 Some people use the colon to carry out the functions of the
semi-colon, especially when they want to emphasise the
contrast between two halves of an antithesis.
2 We use the colon (or the dash, or the colon followed by a dash)
to introduce a list:

The things I remember of Australia are: the smell of gum-
trees after rain; the appallingly bad roads in Melbourne;
the curiously out-of-date trams and gas-stoves and back-
pedalling bicycles; the resolve of the people to have nothing
to do with English ideas such as Daylight Saving; and the
friendliness of the people if you avoided such tactless topics.

3 The colon is also used to introduce a sentence or phrase
explanatory of or amplifying a preceding statement.
The cause of the hold-up soon became clear: two cars had
collided, blocking the road.

The Dash

You will realise, of course, that the hyphen and the dash are
quite different punctuation marks with quite different uses.
Dashes are used as follows:
1 As parenthesis, i.e. for a group of words inserted into a
sentence as an aside:
My mother—she is over eighty—can remember when
every pupil had to pay a penny a week to go to school.
2 To show that the writer has given up the attempt to complete
his sentence grammatically and is either going to end it
quickly or to begin again from the beginning:
I was very much excited at the prospect of school, where
I should meet other boys and girls, and perhaps learn Latin,
and French—our ideas of village schools were vague.

3 To end the sentence with a touch of humour or a wry anticlimax:

> If a swimmer, dressed in a frogman suit and oxygen set,
> swims underwater directly towards a shark, the shark will
> be surprised at the appearance of this unusual underwater
> creature, and will turn away—at least, that is the theory.

4 With a colon to introduce a list or a quotation.

Ending a Sentence

There are several minor problems in how to end a sentence.
An indirect question ends with a full-stop, not a question mark:

> I wonder whether it will snow today.

Sometimes the use of two pairs of quotation marks complicates
your punctuation. Only when a whole sentence is enclosed by
quotation marks should these marks be outside your final full-
stop or query.

> He asked, 'Do you know why Byron left his wife?'
> Did you recognise the quotation about 'the snows of yester-
> year'?
> I asked him, 'How do you translate "raining cats and
> dogs"?'

The last example shows the problem when the phrase quoted
needs its own punctuation marks.

Capital Letters

In English, unlike many other languages, we use capitals for
names of countries, races and languages.

If you are uncertain whether to give a word a capital or not,
the important thing is to be consistent.

Some theorists have said that we use a capital letter for individual examples and a small letter for a word that includes lots
of examples:

> It is a small road off Breck Road.
> We bought some brussels sprouts in Brussels.

Apostrophes

The modern fashion is to write 'Keats's' and to avoid those
phrases where one omits the final apostrophe in order to

prevent an unpleasant hissing sound, as when one says 'for Jesus' sake'. One way to avoid these hissing sibilants is to write 'the poems of Keats' or 'for the sake of Jesus'.

Possessive pronouns such as 'its' and 'yours' and 'hers' do not have apostrophes. The origin of the apostrophe was the false idea that 'the boy's shirt' was short for 'the boy his shirt'. Nobody could suppose that 'its fault' was short for 'it his fault', so 'its' never has an apostrophe, except when it is short for 'it is'.

In writing plurals of unusual nouns such as p's and q's, M.P.s, "buts" and "ifs", etc., use apostrophes only where they seem absolutely essential to the look of the word.

We can say either 'a ten years' imprisonment' or 'a ten-years imprisonment'.

Hyphens

We are very inconsistent about hyphens. For instance, *The Concise Oxford Dictionary* recommends us to write:
  fox-brush, fox-earth, foxglove, foxhole, foxhound, fox-hunt, foxhunter, fox-hunting, foxtail, fox-terrier, and foxtrot.
It is difficult to see any consistency in this. As an American grammarian says: 'If you take hyphens seriously you will surely go mad.' All one can do is to try to be consistent.

Hyphens have four uses. Firstly, there are words that are not separate words such as 'black bird' nor new composite words such as 'blackbird': they belong to a half-way stage, such as 'black-board'.

Secondly, we use hyphens to show that two words have become temporarily united as a single adjective: e.g. copper-coloured hair, government-financed projects.

Thirdly, hyphens show that pairs of adjectives are to be taken together: e.g. red-hot, dark-blue.

Fourthly, there are occasions when some writers think that a word looks less odd with a hyphen: e.g. re-allocate.

TEST 9

A Write a composition of about 450 words on one of the
following topics:

    1 Someone from another country has spent a holiday in
your district. Write, in the first person, an account of
his or her impressions of the holiday

    2 Write a pen-portrait of someone with either an unusual
hobby or an unusual occupation

    3 A novel or book of true adventure that you enjoyed
reading and the reasons why it interested you

    4 The story of a village isolated by severe floods *or* a
heavy fall of snow, and the relief operations that took
place

    5 Write a description of the scene at one of the following
during a very busy period:
        an open-air market, a supermarket, a main-line
railway station, a large factory

B Write about 200 words on one of these:

    1 You have been asked to make arrangements for a
fortnight's holiday for members of your club. Write to
a farmer asking for permission to camp on his land,
giving him all the necessary information about the
holiday and your requirements

    2 Write an article for a magazine that is widely read by
young people on 'A Career to be proud of'

    3 Choose one of the following pairs and explain how the
two items resemble each other and how they differ:
        a symphony orchestra and a military band, an
electric fire and a gas fire, a helicopter and a fighter
plane, a pram and a pushchair

    4 What feature of school life would you most like to see
abolished? Describe this feature and explain clearly
your reasons for wishing to see it abolished

Section II SUMMARY AND COMPREHENSION

    1 Read the following passage and then answer the questions on

it. It is divided into sections merely in order that you can identify the parts of the passage that the questions refer to.

Section A

Treasure-hunting is an activity which combines some of the most irrational and romantic elements in man's make-up. Since sunken treasure is very rarely well documented, it requires an unwavering faith to hunt it.

Above all, treasure appeals to the get-rich-quick instinct.   5
Yet a serious treasure hunt requires years of painstaking research in archives and old newspapers. After 'researching' his treasure, the hunter may spend even longer actually salvaging it. And, after that, there may still be complicated legal wrangles to establish his entitlement to what he has   10
found.

Treasure hunts often end in bankruptcy and even in death. Hunts for a Spanish Armada galleon in Tobermory Bay, Island of Mull, ended in the deaths of two divers. More recently, an expedition to salvage a Spanish treasure ship in   15
the West Indies was successful only at the expense of the death of one of the crew of three. The stakes are higher than on the football pools—and the odds against winning a fortune are probably higher.

But the romance of treasure depends on more than its   20
material value. In the nineteenth century almost 5,000 ships were wrecked on the North American Great Lakes in 20 years alone. Many of them went down with valuable treasure or property; but none of them has made great treasure tales. Like a good wine, treasure is improved by age.   25

Section B

The most famous treasure stories are shrouded in mystery and legend. The mythical treasure of Captain William Kidd, who was hanged in London on a charge of piracy, has been attributed to every known West Indian and Pacific island. There is even a legend that his ship was scuttled somewhere   5
up the Hudson, the crew scattering ashore with what treasure they could. Kidd's fortune is even a favourite subject for
E

visionaries, like the woman who claimed that, in a trance, she had seen the shattered timbers of Kidd's ship and 'bars of massive gold, and precious jewels'.   10

Yet all the historical evidence suggests that Kidd was never a pirate, still less the possessor of any vast wealth. This conclusion has not deterred treasure-hunters. The last two recorded expeditions met with unhappy fates. In 1951, two British companies were formed to undertake expeditions   15 to the South China Sea, complete with the obligatory 'authentic' map, in search of the £120,000 Kidd was alleged to have hoarded. The first set sail from Gosport, flying the skull and crossbones, only to meet the first gale of the season and sink some three days out at sea. The second failed   20 even to complete the hire of a boat.

Another legend, with more basis in fact, has been created around the Spanish Armada galleon which sank in Tobermory Bay in 1588. This has become a Scottish mystery comparable with the Loch Ness Monster. All that is known for   25 certain is that some Spanish ship was sunk in Tobermory after the Armada had been scattered round the coast of Scotland by high winds.

Among the legends about the ship is the story that it was carrying a new royal crown to be worn by King Philip when   30 he entered England as conqueror. Another says that its captain was Isabella, the King's daughter, and that it lingered in the bay for several days because she was so captivated by the laird of Mull.

It is fairly certain that the amount of treasure in the   35 galleon—the popular estimate is £30 million—has been greatly exaggerated. The £1,000 of pewter plate, silver and gold—discovered in Tobermory before the First World War —was probably the captain's personal fortune.

Hunting the galleon has become almost a family sport for   40 the Dukes of Argyll. Attempts by the present Duke to recover the treasure in the 1950s, with the aid of Royal Navy divers, attracted wide interest. Although the site of the wreck was found, little treasure was salvaged. Opinion is hardening that it was nearly all taken away secretly some   45 hundreds of years ago.

Section C

The countless wrecks still awaiting discovery, however, give the treasure-hunter cause for optimism. In the days before banking and credit systems, money had to be moved physically if it was to be spent overseas and this meant that most ships had a fair sum aboard. But the really big cargoes of   5
gold only began crossing the seas when gold mines were discovered in the New World.

At the end of the fifteenth century, less than 100 tons of gold, less than one-tenth of the world's present-day production for a single year, was in circulation throughout Western   10
Europe. From 1500 until about the middle of the nineteenth century around £5,000 million was transported across the world's four great treasure routes. At least £250 million was lost in disasters at sea.

Section D

The greatest treasure-hunting area in the world today—around Florida and the Bahamas, where it is a major industry and tourist attraction—owes its existence to the sometimes tragic journeys of the Spanish treasure ships. Seventy million pounds' worth of treasure lies, still   5
unrecovered, off the Florida coast.

The clear seas of the Bahamas, with their brilliant colours and exotic underwater life, make an ideal environment for diving. But potential treasure-hunters must also face the dangers of sharks, squids, yellow fever, rocks and even   10
hurricanes.

Finding a wreck needs a slice of luck; even modern echo-sounding apparatus does not distinguish between a natural reef and a coral encrusted ship. When it has been located, it may be very difficult to shift the coral.   15

In 1967, an Englishman called Ted Falcon Barker succeeded in salvaging 96 gold coins worth about £3,500, but his voyage was overshadowed by the death of one of his companions. His adventures are told in a book called, significantly, *Devil's Gold*.   20

Section E

Such bizarre adventures are unlikely to occur in the much more scholarly atmosphere of the world's second great treasure-hunting site—the Mediterranean. Here, on the shores of the ancient world, is a storehouse of art and antique, rather than metal, treasures. The hunters are usually nautical archaeologists to some of whom 'treasure-hunter' is a term of abuse and contempt.

Techniques of underwater archaeology have developed only in the last ten to 15 years, as the aqualung has become readily available. In the past archaeologists had to rely on divers who understood little of the technical intricacies of archaeology. It is hoped that modern technological developments may lead to even greater advances in nautical archaeology.

The first archaeologist to sketch plans for an underwater wreck was Peter Throckmorton. From 1960, he worked on a Late Bronze Age ship off Turkey. It was the oldest wreck ever found, dating from 1200 B.C. The cargo contained over a ton of copper and the most important hoard of bronze tools and ingots ever discovered by preclassical archaeologists. They included axes, hoes, picks, a spade, hammers, knives and a mirror.

Analysis suggested that the cargo was Cypriot and the ship and sailors Phoenician. This was an illuminating, historical discovery, since Phoenician merchants were not previously thought to have begun their famous sea trade as early as 1200 B.C.

In such ways, marine archaeology can cast much light on the history of ship construction, on trade-routes and on the daily life of sailors.

Historians are also interested in Armada galleons since many of the details about the invasion force and why it was unsuccessful are still a matter of dispute. Above all, wrecks are a unique source of information about how sailors lived. Much had been written about Admiral Sir Cloudesley Shovell whose flagship, *The Association*, went down off the Isles of Scilly in 1707 but, until the recent discovery of the wreck, very little was known about his crew.

It is here that archaeologists and treasure-hunters may come into conflict. One is interested primarily in the historical value of underwater finds, the other is concerned more with the commercial metal value. Archaeologists, however, are in no position to turn their noses up at treasure. The underwater world is short of money, and treasure may be the only source of funds for a future expedition.   40

45

Section A

1 Which of the following points about treasure-hunting is NOT stressed by this article?

    A it usually involves a wreck about which there is little precise information

    B it arouses a man's noble resolution to defy the sea and weather

    C it raises false hopes of making money easily and quickly

    D it often involves the finder in lawsuits afterwards

    E it may involve the hunter in a variety of dangers

2 The reference to wrecks in the Great Lakes is intended by this writer to stress that

    A older wrecks excite people's imagination more than recent ones do

    B the Great Lakes are unexpectedly dangerous to shipping

    C at times a very large number of ships have been wrecked within the space of a few years

    D some of the greatest sunken treasures have been strangely neglected

    E raising wrecks in the Great Lakes would add to our knowledge of nineteenth-century history

3 'Irrational' (l. 2) means

    A unintelligent

    B unreasonable

    C unthinking

    D uninformed

    E unproved

4 'Romantic elements' (l. 2)

    A concern exciting stories
    B are unrealistic
    C rouse one's instincts
    D appeal to one's imagination
    E make one interested in history

5 'The stakes are higher' (l. 17) means, in this context, that treasure-hunting may

    A bring in more profit
    B necessitate costly organisation
    C cost more lives
    D produce smaller chances of winning
    E cause more excitement

Section B

6 'Shrouded in' (l. 1) means
    A concealed in
    B surrounded by
    C complicated by
    D wrapped in
    E covered in

7 The following words are all used to express a doubt whether Kidd was a pirate with the ONE EXCEPTION of

    A 'famous' (l. 1)
    B 'mythical' (l. 2)
    C 'charge' (l. 3)
    D 'attributed' (l. 4)
    E 'legend' (l. 5)

8 All the following arguments are used to express a doubt whether Kidd was a pirate EXCEPT that

    A his story is shrouded in mystery and legend
    B widely separate parts of the world are suggested as hiding-places for his loot
    C historical evidence suggests that he was not a pirate
    D he was hanged in London on the charge of piracy
    E the exact hiding-place of his treasure is seen in the dreams of fanciful people

9 This writer believes that the galleon which sank in Tobermory Bay

    A is more likely to be a fact than Kidd's treasure was

    B is as difficult to believe in as the Loch Ness Monster

    C is more of a legend than a reality

    D was persuaded to stay in the bay for some days by the King's daughter, Isabella

    E has never produced any treasure at all

10 This writer primarily uses Section B as two striking examples of the

    A widespread human tendency to believe the impossible

    B truth that 'Like a good wine, treasure is improved by age'

    C fact that wrecks rarely yield much treasure

    D tendency of fictitious, romantic stories to develop around stories of treasure trove

    E likelihood of truth to be stranger than fiction

11 'Obligatory' (l. 16) means

    A legally binding

    B politically necessary

    C traditionally expected

    D essential

    E historical

12 'Alleged' (l. 17) means

    A stated without proof

    B unjustifiably supposed

    C usually believed

    D virtually proved

    E normally assumed

Section C

13 Section C, contrasted with Section B,

    A switches to a different period in history
    B switches to a different part of the globe
    C deals with treasure-hunters' grounds for hope
    D uses generalisation rather than example
    E is an aside before the return of the main theme

14 This section suggests that losses of gold at sea have become less frequent since

    A about 1850 because of modern banking methods
    B about 1500 because of improvements in ships
    C about 1500 because of discovery of America and South Africa
    D about 1850 because the total amount of gold ceased to grow rapidly
    E about 1850 because the circulation of gold increased considerably

Section D

15 Choose the one of the following statements about treasure-hunting around Florida and the Bahamas which is NOT true

    A many Spanish treasure-ships were wrecked there
    B treasure-hunting is too difficult to attract tourists
    C it involves a variety of dangers
    D wrecks and reefs are difficult to distinguish from one another
    E the dangers and attractions are summed up in the title of Barker's book

16 'Significantly' (l. 20) indicates that the title of Barker's book is

    A justified
    B ominous
    C full of meaning
    D suggestive
    E typical

Section E

17 Two words in the first paragraph (lines 1–7) that
    stress the transition from the topic of Florida to the
    topic of the Mediterranean are:

    A 'adventures' .... 'ancient'
    B 'unlikely' .... 'shores'
    C 'bizarre' .... 'scholarly'
    D 'such' .... 'unlikely'
    E 'storehouse' .... 'archaeologists'

18 Which of the following words is used in a literal, and
    NOT a metaphorical or figurative sense?

    A 'adventures' (l. 1)
    B 'scholarly' (l. 2)
    C 'storehouse' (l. 4)
    D 'hunters' (l. 5)
    E 'advances' (l. 13)

19 Wrecks in the Mediterranean are most likely to yield

    A important additions to historical knowledge
    B hoards of bronze Phoenician tools
    C new triumphs for new techniques of diving
    D disappointments for archaeologists
    E evidence that shortage of money is seriously
      handicapping underwater archaeology

20 'Primarily' (l. 40) means

    A originally
    B entirely
    C principally
    D almost entirely
    E significantly

Other questions

1 Select and rewrite the arguments which this article puts
forward in defence of treasure-hunting as a serious and
worth-while occupation

2 Quote a significant word or sentence to show that this writer
pokes a certain amount of fun at
    (a) the lack of interest in wrecks in the Great Lakes
    (b) stories about Captain Kidd
    (c) the galleon that sank in Tobermory Bay
Briefly justify your choice

3 Explain the main ways in which scholars who carry out
underwater archaeology are different from other treasure-
hunters

2 Read the following passage and then answer the questions on
it. It is essential to the understanding of the second paragraph to know that it was written in 1938 when war against
Hitler's Germany seemed probable.

Section A

For nearly three hundred years Britain, reconciled to the
Roman system, enjoyed in many respects the happiest, most
comfortable, and most enlightened times its inhabitants
have had. Confronted with the dangers of the frontiers,
the military force was moderate. The Wall was held by the
auxiliaries, with a legion in support at York. Wales was
pinned down by a legion at Chester and another at Caerleon-
on-Usk. In all, the army of occupation numbered less than
forty thousand men, and after a few generations was locally
recruited and almost of purely British birth. In this period,
almost equal to that which separates us from the reign of
Queen Elizabeth I, well-to-do persons in Britain lived
better than they ever did until late Victorian times. From
the year 400 till the year 1900 no one had central heating
and very few had hot baths. A wealthy British-Roman
citizen building a country house regarded the hypocaust
which warmed it as indispensable. For fifteen hundred years
his descendants lived in the cold of unheated dwellings,

mitigated by occasional roastings at gigantic wasteful fires.
Even now a smaller proportion of the whole population   20
dwells in centrally heated houses than in those ancient days.
As for baths, they were completely lost till the middle of
the nineteenth century. In all this long, bleak intervening gap
cold and dirt clung to the most fortunate and highest in the
land.   25

Section B

If a native of Chester in Roman Britain could wake up today
he would find laws which were the direct fulfilment of many
of those he had known. He would find in every village
temples and priests of the new creed which in his day was
winning victories everywhere. Indeed the facilities for   5
Christian worship would appear to him to be far in excess of
the number of devotees. Not without pride would he notice
that his children were compelled to learn Latin if they wished
to enter the most famous universities.

He would find in the public libraries many of the master-   10
pieces of ancient literature, printed on uncommonly cheap
paper and in great numbers. He would find a settled government, and a sense of belonging to a world-wide empire.
He could drink and bathe in the waters of Bath, or if this were
too far he would find vapour baths and toilet conveniences in 15
every city. He would find all his own problems of currency,
land tenure, public morals and decorum presented in a
somewhat different aspect, but still in lively dispute. He
would have the same sense of belonging to a society which
was threatened, and to an imperial rule which had passed its   20
prime. He would have the same gathering fears of some
onslaught by barbarian forces armed with equal weapons to
those of the local legions or auxiliaries.

The most marked changes that would confront him would
be the speed of communications and the volume of printed   25
and broadcast matter. He might find both distressing. But
against these he could set chloroform, antiseptics, and a
more scientific knowledge of hygiene. He would have
longer history books to read, containing worse tales than
those of Tacitus and Dio. Facilities would be afforded to   30

him for seeing 'regions Caesar never knew', from which he would probably return in sorrow and wonder. He would find himself hampered in every aspect of foreign travel, except that of speed. If he wished to journey to Rome, Constantinople, or Jerusalem, otherwise than by sea, a 35 dozen frontiers would scrutinise his entry. He would be called upon to develop a large number of tribal and racial enmities to which he had formerly been a stranger. But the more he studied the accounts of what had happened since the third century the more satisfied he would be not to have 40 been awakened at an earlier time.

Objective Questions

Section A

1 The Britons' attitude to the Roman occupation was that

    A they had welcomed it from the beginning
    B they came to tolerate it grudgingly
    C they came to accept it and helped to prolong it
    D they could not make up their minds about it
    E they continued to resent it

2 Which of the following points about the Roman occupation does the author, Sir Winston Churchill, make?

    i it had several obvious and important disadvantages
    ii it brought happiness to most of the inhabitants
    iii it multiplied comforts such as baths
    iv it needed only a comparatively small army
    v it spread ideas that were tolerant and civilised

    A i, ii, iii and iv
    B i, iii, iv and v
    C i, ii, iv and v
    D ii, iii, iv and v
    E all of them

3 Which ONE of the following facts about the Roman army is NOT stated or implied?

    A no first-class troops were actually stationed *on* the wall between England and Scotland

B the sternest measures to prevent rebellion were taken against the Welsh

C many Britons were recruited in the very early years of the occupation

D towards the end of the occupation most troops were natives of Britain

E very large forces were kept inside the areas most likely to rebel

4 Which ONE of the following points concerning Roman rule is NOT made by Sir Winston?

A it produced more comfort than any other age before (approximately) 1880

B it provided all its rich people with central heating

C it lasted a long time by any standards

D it produced much better hygiene than later ages did

E it made the Britons long for independence

5 Which of the following aspects of Sir Winston's account show that he is thinking mostly about how the rich (not the poor) lived in the past?

i he says how comfortably 'well-to-do persons' lived in Roman Britain

ii he emphasises that every 'wealthy British-Roman citizen' had central heating

iii he mentions the dirt that clung to 'the most fortunate and highest in the land'

iv he says nothing about the hardships of Roman slaves

v he suggests that there were good careers in the Roman army for rich Britons

A i, ii, iii and iv

B i, iii and v

C i, ii, iv and v

D ii, iii, iv and v

E all of them

6   Which ONE of the following remarks about metaphors
    is NOT correct?

    A   in l. 6 the legion at York supports the auxiliaries
    on the wall as a crutch supports a cripple

    B   in l. 7 the legions in Wales are compared to a pin
    holding a butterfly on to a mounting

    C   in l. 19 the way that the cold in houses was reduced
    by huge, but not permanent, fires is compared to
    the way in which a judge's sentence could be
    reduced by the circumstances of the case

    D   In l. 23 the interval between the Roman period
    and modern times is compared to the space made
    in a hedge by missing shrubs

    E   In l. 23 the cheerless period of time between the
    Roman period and today is compared to a cold,
    wet, unprotected area

7   'Indispensable' (l. 17) describes the Roman central-
    heating system as

    A   a luxury
    B   a necessity
    C   an innovation
    D   an interesting experiment
    E   something a little out of date

8   'Equal to' (l. 11) means as

    A   noble as
    B   important as
    C   long as
    D   historical as
    E   famous as

Section B

9   British laws, compared with Roman laws, are

    A   their logical successor
    B   similar to them
    C   a severer version of them
    D   a close imitation of them
    E   an improvement on them

10   Sir Winston Churchill makes all the following points
     about Christianity EXCEPT that

    A in Roman times it was a new religion
    B in Roman times it was gaining converts
    C in Roman times it made progress in the country
       rather than the towns
    D today Christian churches seem numerous
    E today Christian worshippers seem few

11   'Facilities' (l. 5) mean

    A plentiful opportunities
    B favoured privileges
    C helpful provisions
    D ceremonial routines
    E warm enthusiasms

12   The Roman who woke up, like Rip Van Winkle, would
     find all the following results with the ONE EXCEPTION of
     the point that

    A those who wished to enter Oxford and Cambridge
       Universities had to study Latin
    B public libraries contained Latin masterpieces
    C books in Latin were cheap and numerous
    D the government was stable and established
    E fundamental changes had occurred as to what
       were important moral problems

13   The Roman empire, about 250 A.D., and the British
     Empire in 1938 were similar in all the following
     respects EXCEPT that both

    A had plenty of baths and lavatories, at least for the
       rich
    B had similar arguments about finance and law
    C felt that their empire was declining
    D feared that they might be successfully attacked by
       less civilised peoples
    E were protected by large armies

14 'Decorum' (l. 17) means

    A acceptance of tradition
    B dignified behaviour
    C debatable ethics
    D law and order
    E obedience to rules

15 The sentence beginning 'He would find all his own . . .'
(l. 16) shows that Churchill thinks of the Romans as
being fond of

    A quarrelling
    B hair-splitting
    C debating
    D speculating
    E speechifying

16 The re-awakened Roman would

    A welcome the mass of things to read and to hear
       on radio
    B be impressed by advances in medicine
    C find recent history less murderous than Roman
       history
    D enjoy visiting areas like America which the
       Romans never discovered
    E find it easier, in every way, to visit Constantinople
       or Jerusalem

17 The 'facilities' referred to in l. 30 would include all the
following with the ONE EXCEPTION of

    A ocean-going ships
    B air-lines
    C trans-continental railways
    D television
    E charter flights

18 The sentence 'A dozen frontiers would scrutinise his
entry' (l. 36) means that the

    A frontier-guards would examine his passport in
       detail
    B multiplication of frontiers and controls would

make it harder for him to reach these cities

C police of twelve countries would suspect him of having committed a crime

D soldiers at the frontier would extradite him

E obstructions such as the Berlin Wall would keep him out

19 Its 'prime' (l. 21) means its

A beginning

B period of rapid growth

C state of complete perfection

D period of adult vigour

E decline

20 The sentence 'He would be called upon . . . stranger' (l. 36) reminds us that rivalries between French and Germans or between Portuguese and Spaniards

A are fostered today by artificial propaganda

B were felt by the Romans only for complete foreigners

C persisted in so large an empire as the Roman one

D have existed at all times in history

E would have seemed eccentric and exaggerated to the Romans

Other Questions

1 What were the virtues of Roman rule and civilisation that this passage stresses?

2 Why would the imaginary Roman of Section B be glad that he had not woken up earlier?

3 Write a few sentences to prove or disprove each of the following statements about the author

A he is not wholly serious

B he is looking at history from the point of view of the rich, not the poor

C he seems to be revealing a dislike of America

TEST 10

A Write a composition of about 450 words on one of the following topics:

    1 Describe the invention or discovery of the last 100 years which, in your opinion, has made the greatest difference to mankind. Give reasons for your choice

    2 The pleasure of photography or swimming or dancing or cycling

    3 Modern methods of advertising

    4 The story of a missed opportunity and its consequences

    5 The advantages or disadvantages or both of being inquisitive

B Write about 200 words on one of the following:

    1 Your school is arranging a fête or similar function for parents and friends in order to raise money for some new equipment, amenity, or venture. Write a circular letter to parents and friends describing the function and explaining its purpose

    2 Describe clearly how you would make one of the following:

        a table lamp; a kitchen stool; a newspaper or magazine rack; a cake or pudding

    3 There is a proposal to create a traffic-free shopping centre in your town. Write a letter to the local newspaper giving your views on the proposal

    4 Write an account of the work of one of the following: a librarian; a bus or train driver; a district nurse; a professional footballer

Section II SUMMARY AND COMPREHENSION

1 Read the following passage and then answer the questions on it.

    Long before the age of man, insects inhabited the earth—a group of extraordinarily varied and adaptable beings. Over the course of time since man's advent, a small percentage of the more than half a million species of insects have come

into conflict with human welfare in two principal ways: 5
as competitors for the food supply, and as carriers of human
disease.

Disease-carrying insects become important where human
beings are crowded together, especially under conditions
where sanitation is poor, as in times of natural disaster or   10
war or in situations of extreme poverty and deprivation.
Then control of some sort becomes necessary. It is a sobering
fact, however, that the method of massive chemical control
has had only limited success, and also threatens to worsen
the very conditions it is intended to curb.   15

Under primitive agricultural conditions the farmer had
few insect problems. These arose with the intensification of
agriculture—the devotion of immense acreages to a single
crop. Such a system set the stage for explosive increases in
specific insect populations. Single-crop farming does not   20
take advantage of the principles by which nature works; it
is agriculture as an engineer might conceive it to be. Nature
has introduced great variety into the landscape, but man has
displayed a passion for simplifying it. Thus he undoes the
built-in checks and balances by which nature holds the species   25
within bounds. One important natural check is a limit on the
amount of suitable habitat for each species. Obviously, then,
an insect that lives on wheat can build up its population to
much higher levels on a farm devoted to wheat than on one
in which wheat is intermingled with other crops to which   30
the insect is not adapted.

The same thing happens in other situations. A generation or
more ago, the towns of large areas of the United States
lined their streets with the noble elm tree. Now the beauty
they hopefully created is threatened with complete destruction   35
as disease sweeps through the elms, carried by a beetle that
would have only a limited chance to build up large populations
and to spread from tree to tree if the elms were only occasional
trees in a richly diversified planting.

(a) Explain in your own words the ways in which insects
    have caused difficulties to man
(b) When does this author think it is justifiable to reduce
    the numbers of insects?

(c) Explain in your own words the change in farming methods mentioned in this passage

(d) Why did this change in farming methods cause a new problem for farmers?

(e) What does the writer mean by the words: 'Thus he undoes the built-in checks and balances by which nature holds the species within bounds'? (ll. 24–26)

(f) Explain in your own words how the elm trees in America illustrate the writer's point in this passage

(g) Give the meaning in the passage of the following words: adaptable (l. 2), advent (l. 3), curb (l. 15), primitive (l. 16), conceive (l. 22), habitat (l. 27), intermingled (l. 30), diversified (l. 39)

Objective Questions

For each of the following questions choose the answer that seems most correct, and write down the letter that represents your correct answer:

1 This author's attitude to insects is that they

    A are a major threat to mankind
    B fill her with repulsion
    C will take mankind's place on earth
    D are a danger only under circumstances that man should prevent
    E reveal the triumph of an adaptable species

2 'Adaptable' (l. 2) stresses the fact that insects

    A are a major threat to man
    B were created long before man
    C are found in certain climates only
    D can adjust themselves to different environments
    E are unpredictable in their behaviour

3 'Advent' (l. 3) means

    A arrival
    B development
    C civilisation
    D evolution
    E growth

4   'A sobering fact' (l. 12) is one which makes us less

    A   drunk
    B   reckless
    C   optimistic
    D   visionary
    E   scientific

5   This author insists that a massive use of chemical insecticides

    A   is very successful
    B   has disappointingly small effect
    C   is justified as an attack on extreme poverty
    D   reduces consumption of alcohol
    E   is a necessary form of scientific control

6   'Curb' (l. 15) means

    A   reduce
    B   restrain
    C   check
    D   erode
    E   improve

7   'Primitive' (l. 16) means belonging to

    A   an age that uses little machinery
    B   the early stages in man's development
    C   the original, natural state of the world
    D   people using unsophisticated techniques
    E   conditions that are unhealthy

8   To keep down the number of insects and the danger from them this author prefers to

    A   use chemical sprays
    B   invent new chemicals
    C   avoid planting elms
    D   plant a variety of crops in one area
    E   develop new varieties of crops that resist insects

9 To this author 'war' (l. 11) is

    A a major threat to humanity
    B only a small part of her argument
    C a time when insects eat too much of man's food
    D a cause of extreme poverty
    E a necessary form of biological control

10 When man began to grow large quantities of the same crop in one area, this

    A greatly increased the numbers of certain insects
    B greatly increased the numbers of all insects
    C slightly increased the numbers of certain insects
    D greatly lengthened the life of certain insects
    E spread the danger from insects over a wider area

11 'Important' (l. 26) means

    A effective
    B worrying
    C fatally dangerous
    D momentous and threatening
    E prolific and numerous

12 'Checks' (l. 25) means

    A rebuffs
    B repulses
    C reverses
    D restraints
    E controls

13 'Bounds' (l. 26) means

    A jumps
    B rises in number
    C frontiers
    D limits
    E territories

14 'Conceive it to be' (l. 22) means

    A formulate it in the mind
    B exaggerate it
    C create it
    D think of it
    E find words to describe it

15 'Habitat' (l. 27) means the area where a species
    A breeds
    B lives
    C thrives
    D migrates
    E feeds

16 Mixed farming reduces the
    A beauty of the landscape
    B variety of insects
    C danger from insects
    D balance of nature
    E adaptability of insects

17 The point of the last paragraph is that it
    A gives an exception to the general rule
    B shows that the author is interested in trees
    C gives another example to reinforce a point made
       before
    D stresses the adaptability of insects
    E stresses the especial vulnerability of elms

18 The last paragraph
    A does not make it very plain whether both the beetle
       and the disease attack other trees besides elms
    B suggests that other agencies, beside this beetle,
       spread disease from tree to tree
    C is quite sure that the beetle would not pass from
       elm to elm if other types of tree intervened
    D illustrates the need to plant a young tree whenever
       an old one is felled
    E stresses the necessity of an overall blue-print for
       replanning cities

19 'Richly diversified' (l. 39) means
    A thoroughly varied
    B expensively modified
    C altered so as to provide one tree for a rich town
       and another for a poor town
    D given exotic varieties
    E given new breeds in a costly manner

20 Which ONE of the following points is NOT made by the article in discussing insects?

    A insects which carry disease are very dangerous only when people are unusually crowded together

    B attempts to control insects by using chemical pesticides do not really solve the problem

    C insects did not become a serious threat till immense areas began to specialise in growing one crop

    D very few of the various types are serious dangers to mankind

    E estimates of rises in insect populations are always much exaggerated

2 Read the following passage and then answer the questions on it.

The passage criticises the belief of the English poet, Wordsworth, that one can understand God by looking at the scenery He created.

In the neighbourhood of latitude fifty north, and for the last hundred years or thereabouts, it has been an axiom that Nature is divine and morally uplifting. For good Wordsworthians—and most serious-minded people are now Wordsworthians, either by direct inspiration or at second-hand—a walk in the country is the equivalent of going to church, a tour through Westmorland is as good as a pilgrimage to Jerusalem. To commune with the fields and waters, the woodlands and the hills, is to commune with the visible manifestations of the 'Wisdom and Spirit of the Universe'.

The Wordsworthian who exports this pantheistic worship of Nature to the tropics is liable to have his religious convictions somewhat rudely disturbed. Nature, under a vertical sun, and nourished by the equatorial rains, is not at all like that chaste, mild deity who presides over the prettiness and the cosy sublimities of the Lake District. The worst that Wordsworth's goddess ever did to him was to make him realise, in the shape of 'a huge peak, black and huge', the existence of 'unknown modes of being'. He seems to imagine that this was the worst Nature could do. A few weeks in Malaya or Borneo would have undeceived him.

Wandering in the hothouse darkness of the jungle, he would not have felt so serenely certain of those 'Presences of Nature', those 'Souls of Lonely Places', which he was in the habit of worshipping on the shore of Windermere and Rydal. 25 The sparse inhabitants of the equatorial forest are all believers in devils. When one has visited the places where they live, it is difficult not to share their faith. The jungle is marvellous, fantastic, beautiful; but it is also terrifying, it is also profoundly sinister. There is something in the character of 30 great forests which is foreign, appalling, fundamentally and utterly inimical to intruding man.

It is not the sense of solitude that distresses the wanderer in equatorial jungles; it is too much company. To us who live beneath a temperate sky and in the age of Henry Ford, the 35 worship of Nature comes almost naturally. It is easy to love a feeble and already conquered enemy. But an enemy with whom one is still at war, an unconquered, unconquerable, ceaselessly active enemy—No! one does not, one should not, love *him*. One respects him, perhaps; one has a salutary fear of 40 him; and one goes on fighting. In our latitudes the hosts of Nature have mostly been vanquished and enslaved. Some few detachments, it is true, still hold the field against us. There are wild woods and mountains, marshes and heaths, even in England. But they are only there on sufferance 45 because we have chosen out of our good pleasure to leave them their freedom. It has not been worth our while to reduce them to slavery. We love them because we are the masters, because we know that at any moment we can overcome their fellows. The inhabitants of the tropics have no 50 such comforting reasons for adoring the sinister forces which hem them in on every side.

Paragraph One

1 'An axiom' (l. 2) is

    A a widely accepted belief
    B a truth requiring no proof
    C an abstract theory
    D an obsession dogmatically accepted
    E an essential part of orthodox Christianity

2　In this first paragraph Huxley

    A　shows that he agrees with Wordsworth

    B　exaggerates Wordsworth's ideas in order to ridicule them gently

    C　stresses the connections between Wordsworth's ideas and Christianity

    D　is surprised that people regard a country walk as a way of worshipping God

    E　openly and directly rejects Wordsworth's ideas

3　Wordsworthians believe that beautiful landscapes are

    A　outward signs of God

    B　vague expressions of a general goodness

    C　homes of nymphs and spirits

    D　inspirations for day dreams

    E　sources of cultural enlightenment

4　To become a Wordsworthian 'by direct inspiration' (l. 5) is to do so by

    A　visiting the Lake District

    B　listening to people who share his beliefs

    C　reading Wordsworth's poems

    D　receiving promptings from God

    E　going to church

5　According to Huxley (ll. 6–10) most people regard a tour through Westmorland as

    A　merely innocent relaxation

    B　a way of getting nearer to God

    C　as exciting as a visit to Palestine

    D　a sort of religious visit to Wordsworth's birthplace

    E　a journey made along with people of similar belief

6　'To commune with' (l. 9) means to

    A　talk intimately with

    B　gain knowledge of

    C　celebrate a sacrament with

    D　establish a close relationship with

    E　learn the truth about

7   'Visible manifestations' (l. 9) are

    A   outward expressions
    B   obvious pieces of evidence
    C   noticeable exhibitions
    D   sacred revelations
    E   evident affirmations

Paragraph Two

8   The main idea of this paragraph is that Wordsworth's
  ideas

    A   lead inhabitants of the tropics to worship a more
       exotic idea of Nature
    B   imply a belief in devils as well as in good spirits
    C   will ultimately appear to contradict themselves
    D   are less convincing in the tropics than in England
    E   show how incomplete is man's control over Nature

9   This same main idea could be expressed rather differently
  by saying that in the tropics Nature appears as

    A   a force that punishes man for his misdeeds
    B   an evil power in a way she does not appear in
       England
    C   a spirit inhabiting lonely places
    D   something that is fantastically beautiful
    E   a goddess of whose deity Wordsworth was
       certainly confident

10 You should be able to deduce that a 'pantheistic worship
  of Nature' (l. 11) means the belief that

    A   God can be worshipped in all his creations
    B   Nature is fundamentally good and kind
    C   in Nature good and evil are equally balanced
    D   God made man in His own image
    E   God is relevant only to a temperate climate

11 In the Lake District Nature appears to be all of the
following with the ONE EXCEPTION of

    A pure
    B gentle
    C comfortable
    D inspiring
    E ominous

12 The inhabitants of the equatorial forests

    A live crowded together in populous places
    B are ashamed of their secret superstitions
    C are cheerfully adapted to local conditions
    D associate the jungle with evil spirits
    E are convinced that Nature is a fruitful, generous
goddess

13 For an inhabitant of a tropical forest to believe in devils
seems to Huxley to be

    A a natural reaction to the forest's menacing
appearance
    B proof that he is a prey to irrational fears
    C the result of the intense steamy heat
    D an idea that is less noble than Wordsworth's faith
    E a surprising and odd fact to recall

14 Huxley intends all the following words to stress the bad
aspects of tropical forests with the ONE EXCEPTION of

    A 'fantastic' (l. 29)
    B 'terrifying' (l. 29)
    C 'sinister' (l. 30)
    D 'appalling' (l. 31)
    E 'inimical' (l. 32)

15 'Intruding' (l. 32) reminds us that in tropical forests man

    A is on the retreat
    B does not seem to belong
    C loses his self-confidence
    D erects superstitions
    E tries to extend cultivation

Paragraph Three

16   'It is too much company' (l. 34) suggests that in the
      tropics man is accompanied by all the following EXCEPT

      A mosquitoes, snakes, alligators, etc.
      B luxurious creepers and flowers
      C shrubs and other forms of undergrowth
      D fears of devils and evil forces
      E fellow human beings

17   The sentence about beliefs beneath a temperate sky and
      in the age of Henry Ford (l. 35) introduces

      A an apparent contradiction
      B more variety
      C a comparison
      D a contrast
      E an aside

18   All the following contain the same metaphor as one
      another with the ONE EXCEPTION of

      A 'It is easy to love a feeble . . . enemy' (l. 36)
      B 'an enemy with whom one is still at war' (l. 37)
      C 'The hosts of Nature have been mostly vanquished'
         (l. 41)
      D 'Some few detachments still hold the field against
         us' (l. 43)
      E 'But they are only there on sufferance' (l. 45)

19   Huxley says the wilder parts of England

      A are still very beautiful
      B can still be dangerous
      C make us receptive to Wordsworth's ideas
      D could easily be removed
      E still defy the march of urbanisation

20   All the following contain the same metaphor as one
      another with the ONE EXCEPTION of

      A 'wild woods and mountains' (l. 44)
      B 'to leave them their freedom' (l. 46)
      C 'to reduce them to slavery' (l. 48)
      D 'we are the masters' (l. 48)
      E 'adoring the sinister forces' (l. 51)

21 'salutary' (l. 40) means

    A beneficial
    B suitable
    C natural
    D unconscious
    E cautious

The passage as a whole

22 A suitable title would be

    A The Jungle is Neutral
    B Wordsworth in the Tropics
    C From Gentle Grasmere to Frightening Forests
    D Is Nature Christian in the Tropics?
    E Daffodils or Devils

Other Questions

1 Show how the first paragraph repeats Wordsworth's ideas, but hints at criticisms of them to be made in later paragraphs

2 Explain the point made in the second paragraph, that one develops a different attitude to Nature in the tropics from that which one has in England

3 To what extent does the first sentence of the third paragraph express a different idea from that of the rest of the paragraph? To what extent does the paragraph possess a unity?

4 Explain the meaning of the following sentence, and show that you follow how it uses an extended metaphor:

    'Some few detachments, it is true, still hold the field against us.' (ll. 42–3)

5 Explain the appropriateness of the following groups of words

    (i) that chaste, mild deity who presides over the prettiness and cosy sublimities of the Lake District (ll.15–16)
    (ii) foreign, appalling, fundamentally and utterly inimical to intruding man (ll. 31–2)
    (iii) an unconquered, unconquerable, ceaselessly active enemy (ll. 38–9)

CHAPTER NINE

Errors in Writing

NOTES

I COMMON ERRORS WITH VERBS

(a) *Shall and Will* The straightforward future tense of the verb *to be* is as follows:

I shall be	we shall be
you (singular) will be	you (plural) will be
he will be	they will be

But this is complicated by the existence of another verb 'I will', which means 'I am quite determined to' or 'I promise to':

I will	we will
you shall	you shall
he shall	he shall

Everyone knows the joke of the Irishman who could not learn this difficult piece of grammar (which the Irish and the Americans ignore). He fell into the water and shouted:

'I will drown and no-one shall save me.'

The only man who heard his cries was an English grammarian who interpreted this to mean that the man was resolved to commit suicide, and so let him drown.

It is customary to apply the same rule to the conditional tense, and so it is correct to write:

I should be grateful if you would send me details.

(b) *The Split Infinitive* In most languages the infinitive consists of one word only. For instance, 'to love' becomes 'aimer' in French. In English, however, the infinitive is not usually one word:

I was sorry *to miss* that television programme.

But because *to miss* is thought of as a unit, it is usual not to split it by putting a word in the middle of the infinitive. You would split it if you wrote:

To carelessly miss an open goal is unforgivable in a footballer.

But splitting an infinitive is a small fault, and sometimes in trying to avoid it you produce a cumbersome, muddled sentence.

(c) *Sitting and Standing* Two past tenses are sometimes confused. Different forms of the past tenses of these verbs are:

I sat .... I was sitting
she stood .... she was standing

It is wrong to muddle these and to write:

I was sat   *or*   she was stood.

(d) *Passed and Past* 'Passed' is the past tense of the verb 'to pass':

I passed by your window.

It is also a past participle:

I have often passed that church.

'Past' is (i) a noun meaning 'time that has passed':
She cherishes her memories of the past.

(ii) an adjective meaning 'belonging to the past':
past events, past participle, past tense.

(iii) a preposition (joining a noun or pronoun to the rest of the sentence):
She walked past me.

(e) *Must and Ought* 'Ought' is an old form of part of the verb 'to owe'. It is now used to indicate a sense of obligation and has only one tense-form. It is followed by a present infinitive when its sense is present or future:

I ought to be at work now.

I ought to go to a meeting in Manchester tomorrow.

It is followed by the perfect infinitive when it refers to the past:

I ought to have cleaned the car yesterday.

Two confusions arise:

1 Because in speech we slide over the infinitive 'to have done', saying 'to've done', some students confuse 'have' with 'of'. But although the pronunciation is similar, their meanings are very different:

I am a man *of* few words.

You ought not to *have* been so hasty . . .

2 People try to form the usual interrogative and negative parts of 'ought' by using *do* and *did,* as one can with normal verbs:

Do I like bananas? Did I like bananas before I met you?

But because *ought* is a defective verb (one that you can only use certain parts of) you cannot say:

Do you ought to like bananas? I did not ought to like bananas.

You must say:

Ought you to like bananas? I ought not to like bananas.

Must and Should are also defective verbs. 'Must' has no past tense, so you have to say:

I had to go yesterday.

Both 'must' and 'should' are often followed by 'have':

I must have left my book next door.

I should have seized my opportunity yesterday.

(f) *Verb and Subject* A verb must agree in number with its subject. But this is not always as easy as it sounds. Sometimes the verb is incorrectly attracted by a second noun that intervenes between the true subject and the verb:

A row of black and white houses, attractive to tourists, have been reconstructed.

The verb, which ought to agree with the subject 'row', has been incorrectly lured into the plural by the intervening words 'houses' and 'tourists'. Possibly it is best to avoid this type of error by reframing the sentence to keep the plurals together:

The black and white houses, attractive to tourists, have been reconstructed and now form an impressive row.

Two singular subjects connected by *either . . . or* require a singular verb:

Either Margaret or Janet is at home.

Other words that are always followed by a singular verb include *each, neither, everyone, anyone*:

Neither of the books is suitable.

Everyone is to go to his home.

In dealing with a collective noun (e.g. herd, flock), we can

F

treat it either as singular or as plural (whichever seems the more sensible), but having decided, we must be consistent. We must not write:

> Manchester United *has* bought a new outside-right, and so *they* should do better in future.

(g) *Unrelated Participles* The following sentences are obviously correct:

> Looking at the thrilling television play, he forgot to make the telephone call.
> Condemned by all the critics, the record has nevertheless climbed high in the charts.

Both sentences begin with a participle, a word that is partly verb and partly adjective. Both participles agree with the eventual main subject of the sentences. But let us consider these sentences:

> Coming out of the cinema, the crowd saw the snow falling rapidly.
> Coming out of the cinema, the snow was falling rapidly.

The first is correct, but the second is incorrect as there is no word for the participle 'coming' to refer to and so it is said to be unrelated.

However, it is usual to regard this next sentence as correct:

> Considering his age, he is still very active.

Here 'considering' is regarded as a preposition; similarly it is usual to accept 'regarding', 'owing to', 'concerning' and 'failing' as prepositions.

Grammarians argue whether it is correct to use 'due to' as this sort of preposition. It is correct to write

> The hold-up was due to the snow.

But many grammarians think it wrong to write

> Due to the rain the cricket match was abandoned.

They say that 'due to' is an adjective, not a preposition, and needs to describe a word such as 'postponement' that is not actually used. 'Owing to the rain . . .' is more correct.

II OTHER ERRORS

(a) *Noun as Adjective* One of the ways in which English differs from Latin or French is that a noun can quite properly be used as an adjective. We can say:

The Liverpool forwards were off form today.

Here we use the noun 'Liverpool' as an adjective to qualify 'forwards'. Similarly we talk of 'mountain slopes' or 'an island paradise'. But although we may do this if the noun is simple and fits into the rhythm of the sentence, it sounds unnatural if we use a complicated noun in this way or a noun-adjective that destroys the rhythm of the sentence. We find this in scientific writing sometimes:

> Kretschmer's delineation of the schizoid and the cycloid reaction types will long remain a masterpiece of empirical psychology.

Newspaper headlines also illustrate this ugly overuse of nouns as adjectives:

> Insanity rules critic
>
> Hanging probe names soon
>
> April opening for stately home tax deal

Journalists write 'The fats position will be improved' when they mean 'more fats will be available' or 'The eggs position exceeds all expectation' when they mean 'hens are laying more eggs'. It sounds natural to write about 'nursery schools' but to go one stage further and to write 'nursery schools provision' is to destroy the natural rhythm of English. This example illustrates the general advice one must give—that we all use many nouns as adjectives, but we must limit this use to nouns that are simple, unaccompanied by adjectives, and fit naturally into the rhythm of the sentence.

(b) *Problems of Case* In many languages grammar is greatly complicated by the fact that a noun, adjective, or pronoun may change its ending according to its function in the sentence. But while English has almost shed these inflexions, traces remain in our pronouns, where we have different endings for cases:

Nominative:	I	he	she	who	we	they
Accusative:	me	him	her	whom	us	them
Genitive:	mine	his	hers	whose	ours	theirs

All English prepositions are followed by a noun or pronoun in the accusative case: against whom, with me, about him, before them, between you and me, except her and me.

Should we write 'It is I' or 'It is me'?

In the past it was argued that the verb 'to be' must be followed by a nominative complement; thus 'It is I' is correct. But a more modern argument says that we need an emphatic pronoun in a sentence like that, and that just as the French would say 'c'est moi', so we need the more emphatic 'It is me'. The second argument seems a better one, and is in keeping with instinctive usage. On formal occasions, it is better to avoid both methods; the careful writer would find a way to express himself in words that will not seem ungrammatical to the old or unnatural to the young. Another problem of case arises with 'than I' and 'as we'. Grammarians insist that 'as' and 'than' are not prepositions to be followed by the accusative case, but conjunctions to be followed by a clause, even if this is not completed. The grammarian would write:

She is as tall as I. He is older than I.

Many of us, in speaking, would say incorrectly:

She is as tall as me. He is older than me.

If you cannot avoid using this form of sentence it is better to complete the sentences, and write:

She is as tall as I am. He is older than I am.

III ERRORS OF STYLE AND USE OF WORDS

Position of 'only'. Suppose you write: 'The Flemings will only accept French as a foreign language'. This might be condemned as ambiguous. It can mean:

(i) they will *accept* it, as one takes unpleasant medicine, but will not welcome it. (To other Belgians it is their native tongue.)

(ii) they will accept it only if they are allowed to class it as a foreign language.

If your meaning was the first, you could have made it clearer by using different words:

'The Flemings grudgingly tolerate French, but regard it as a foreign language.'

If your meaning was the second, it would be clearer if 'only' was nearer to 'foreign':

The Flemings will accept French only as a foreign language.

While it is possible to be too fussy about the position of 'only',
it is sometimes necessary to be careful how you position it
to make your meaning clear:

She only shot her lover when he deserted her.

This could mean any one of three things unless you move the
word 'only': she only shot him, she did not torture him; she did
not shoot him until he deserted her; or she only shot him (on
those occasions) when he left her.

Unnecessary Prepositions One of the sillier of Americans' habits of
speech is that they use unnecessary prepositions. They do not
meet a friend; they meet up with him. They are not content to
check their facts; they check up on them. When they have
missed their turn, they say that they have missed out on it.
In writing English, omit unnecessary prepositions.

Affect and Effect There is a common verb 'to affect' meaning to
change or have an influence on: 'The weather affects our
tempers'.

There is also a common noun 'effect', meaning result:

The weather has an effect on our tempers.

When the rain affects the harvest, it has an adverse effect
on the farmer's prosperity.

These common uses of 'affect' and 'effect' are somewhat
complicated by two quite different meanings of the two words.
'Affect' also means 'to pretend to have, to put on':

Although he was born in Lancashire, he affects a southern
accent.

There is also another verb 'effect', meaning 'to achieve or
accomplish'.

The use of the tractor has effected a great advance in
farming.

Literally 'Literally' means the opposite of 'figuratively' or
'metaphorically'. It is therefore ridiculous to use it with a
metaphor. If you say

He literally exploded with rage

you mean that he was blown to pieces, as by a bomb. Equally
absurd are:

He literally tore his hair.

The tennis player literally wiped the floor with her opponent.

Less and Fewer We use 'less' for a quantity or amount—less coal, less trouble, less unemployment; but we use 'fewer' for numbers—fewer spectators, fewer unemployed, fewer quarrels. We eat less bacon and fewer eggs.

Disinterested This word is often misused today. Cabinet ministers are as likely to use it wrongly as schoolboys. The confusion, is due to 'interest' having several meanings. Among these are:

(i) a feeling of wanting to know about something or to take part in it;

(ii) a private advantage, profit or benefit.

When you have the first sort of interest, you are *interested* in a hobby or book or film. The opposite of this is *uninterested*. When a town councillor has an interest of the second type, such as when he is a builder likely to profit from some scheme the town council is proposing, it is usual for him not to vote on the matter, and not to speak in its favour unless he has first declared his *interest* in it. Thus an 'interested party' is a person likely to gain or lose personally from some decision. The opposite of this is 'disinterested' or 'neutral' or 'impartial'.

The usual error is to use 'disinterested' where 'uninterested' is needed. For a judge to be uninterested in the case he was trying would be regrettable; for him to be disinterested would be essential.

TEST 11

Section I TOPICS FOR COMPOSITION

A Write an essay of about 450 words on one of the following topics:

   1 A balanced description of the town or community in which you live, intended for a stranger of your own age who is hoping to come to live there

   2 The menace of noise in modern life

   3 Day-dreaming

   4 The encroachment of towns on the countryside

   5 Losing one's temper

   6 Write a passage that might figure in a novel. In it a crowd suddenly begins to disperse

   7 Describe the person, place or event by which you have been most influenced

B

   1 Explain how to do one of the following well, assuming that your reader has tried to do it but is not as good at it as you are: grow roses; iron a shirt; cook roast beef with Yorkshire pudding and two vegetables; mend a puncture in a bicycle tyre; revive a drowning person; bowl a googly; find in your library the book *Cooper's Creek* by Alan Moorehead about an incident in Australian exploration; fill in a football coupon

   2 Write a letter to a newspaper urging Britain to make more use of canals. You may, if you like, use the following points: many of them need repairs, everywhere south of Ripon, mostly still navigable, neglected by railways who bought them out, Inland Waterways Executive (1948–62) missed the opportunity to modernise them, many power-stations use water from canals or rivers but do not receive coal by water, unique opportunities for holidays, amusing experiences working locks, good way to see England, various local associations busy modernising them

   3 State the case for a particular charity as though writing the words of an appeal to be broadcast

Section II SUMMARY AND COMPREHENSION

1 Read the following passage and then write three summaries, each of 80 words, (a) stating the ways in which the details of the problem of derelict land have changed in recent years (b) explaining how much harm is done to certain districts, indirectly as well as directly, by spoils from mining (c) the special arguments for reclaiming land of type A

Britain's Wealth and Power were built, and to a large extent still rest, on the exploitation and industrial use of her mineral resources. This is a process which inevitably makes a mess of the land. Our forebears, for the most part, left the mess as it was: either they did not mind it, or they found the task of cleaning it up too difficult or too costly. The legacy of their neglect is that today, in England and Wales alone, more than 150,000 acres lie derelict.

We in our generation have more regard for the beauty of our countryside, more control over what is done to it and a much greater technical capacity to repair the ravages it suffers. We try to confine its despoilment by mineral extraction and industrial development within the bounds of need and we oblige the extractive industries to make good most of the damage they cannot avoid doing. Yet each succeeding year sees a larger addition to the total acreage of land that has been worked out and left unproductive. The spread of dereliction has now reached at least 3,500 acres a year.

The area blighted by this creeping canker is, of course, much more extensive still. Our derelict acreage is made up of tens of thousands of separate patches. In some parts of the country these patches are sparsely scattered, but in the older industrial regions (where most of them lie) they are often close together. Where one acre in ten is laid waste, the whole landscape is disfigured: and such areas between them cover something like two thousand square miles. Throughout much of South Lancashire and South Wales, Tyneside and the Black Country, the face of the earth is riddled with abandoned mineral workings, pocked with subsidence, gashed with quarries, littered with disused plant

and piled high with stark and sterile banks of dross and
debris, spoil and slag.

These deformities of nature do more than mar the view.
Their grim desolation dulls the spirit—as their dust and   35
fumes defile the fabric—of the human settlements that straggle
among them. Smouldering pit heaps foul the air, poisonous
chemicals pollute the waterways, and treacherous pits
endanger the lives of adventurous children. Neglected
wastes breed vermin and disease. Their very existence   40
fosters slovenliness and vandalism, invites the squatters'
shack, and engenders a 'derelict land mentality' that can never
be eradicated until the mess itself has been cleared up.
Dereliction, indeed, breeds a brutish insensibility, bordering
on positive antagonism, to the life and loveliness of the   45
natural landscape it has supplanted. It debases as well as
disgraces our civilisation.

'Where there's muck there's money' was the glib cliché
that comforted our forebears' consciences. Today we are
beginning to see that dirt, dereliction and decay are major   50
obstacles to the future prosperity of our older industrial
centres. We have undertaken to abate the pollution of the
atmosphere in these 'black areas'. But as yet we have made
no systematic effort to tackle the mess that sullies the earth.

Some of the land laid waste by industry, now as always, is   55
continually being restored or reclaimed for development
because it pays to restore or reclaim it. Such land presents
no problem. Our concern is only with those derelict areas
which are likely to remain offensive for a long time unless
we are prepared to go to some trouble and expense to deal   60
with them now simply because they are offensive. These unwanted sites can be divided into three broad categories.

A: about 36,000 acres in urban areas where undeveloped
land is getting scarce and expensive. Though not immedi-
ately in demand, all sites in this category are likely to be   65
wanted for some form of development at some time in the
next half-century. But it will not be financially profitable to
reclaim them for development until there is no more
undeveloped farmland to be had in their vicinity at a price
which is lower than the cost of reclaiming them. Land is   70
this category may be subdivided as follows:

(i) about 24,000 acres of spoil-heaps, abandoned buildings and miscellaneous dereliction. We should reclaim these for urban development as fast as the demand for it allows, instead of prematurely urbanising what is left of the open country in their neighbourhood. 75

(ii) about 12,000 acres of holes in the ground which are likely to be needed in due course for the tipping of town wastes, and which could thereafter be economically developed as sites for housing or playing fields. We should hold these in reserve for refuse disposal, which would otherwise spread over virgin farmland. In the meanwhile they need 'cosmetic' treatment. 80 85

B: something like 114,000 acres of industrial dereliction in less populous areas where there is no foreseeable prospect of large-scale development. These should be visually redeemed by such grassing or tree-planting as is needed to make them merge into the surrounding countryside. 90

C: the annual net addition to our derelict acreage. Out of some 12,000 acres a year now being taken for the working of minerals and the tipping of spoil and waste, about 8,500 are afterwards restored to farming use by the operators in compliance with the conditions attached to their planning consents. The remaining 3,500 are not restored. These should likewise be visually redeemed by landscaping of a kind that goes beyond mere 'cosmetic' titivation, if possible while the process of extraction is going on. 95

Reclamation schemes vary widely in cost, but such experience as we have suggests that if we undertook to bring all the land in Category A(i) back into some kind of use as soon as possible, instead of waiting till it was economically ripe for urban development, we should incur an average gross outlay of about £700 an acre. Assuming that the market value of the reclaimed land continued, as heretofore, to average about £220 an acre, the net cost would come to about £480 an acre. Temporary 'cosmetic' treatment for the holes in Category A(ii) might add another quarter of a million. If we went on to rehabilitate visually, by afforestation or by establishing permanent grass, all the 100 105 110 derelict land in Category B (which is unlikely ever to be wanted for urban development), the net cost would probably work out, on the basis of past experience, at an average of about £55 an acre, or £6¼ millions in sum. A comprehensive   115 twenty-year programme for the renewal of all the land left derelict by past industrial activities would therefore require a net outlay of nearly £900,000 a year.

Objective Questions

  1 The first paragraph stresses that some disfigurement of the landscape by mining

     A could have been prevented easily

     B cannot be avoided in the long run

     C was worse in the past than it is today

     D increases our industrial wealth and prosperity

     E comes from failing to reclaim land that need not have stayed derelict

  2 If we compare the spread of derelict land today (lines 9–19) and contrast it with the past, the most important factor is that

     A the acreage of unproductive land gets even larger

     B more efforts are made today to preserve beauty

     C our increased technical capacity reduces the problem

     D the law forces mines and quarries to restore some derelict land

     E the law restricts the area to be spoiled by mining

  3 We can make the following deductions about the 'area blighted' (l. 20)

     i this includes land less badly ruined than that 'worked out and left unproductive'

     ii this includes land not referred to by this writer's phrase 'the spread of dereliction'

     iii it includes patches of derelict land that are not continuous

     iv the level of the land has fallen below its original level because of mining v it is mostly found in the areas where industry thrived in earlier centuries

A i, ii and iii only
B i, ii, iii and iv only
C i, iii and iv only
D i, ii, iii and v only
E all of them

4 In talking about 'derelict acreage' (l. 21) this article is referring to the following

   i piles of debris left from mining
   ii areas ruined by subsidence caused by mining
   iii areas ruined by quarrying
   iv disused machinery from old mines
   v marshy land not properly drained

A i, ii and iv
B i, iii and v
C i, ii, iii and iv
D i, ii and v
E all of them

5 'Sparsely' (l. 23) means

A unevenly
B thinly
C widely
D scarcely
E erratically

6 The phrase 'These deformities of nature' (l. 34) has the following effects: it

   i seems an odd phrase, since the deformities are caused by industry
   ii accuses industry of providing mineral ores in a way that makes ugliness inevitable
   iii bridges the change of subject from one paragraph to the other
   iv prepares the reader for a list of the ill-effects of dereliction
   v reminds us of natural deformities such as oaks struck by lightning

A i, ii, iii and iv
B i, iii and iv
C i, iii, iv and v
D ii, iii and iv
E iii, iv and v

7   All the following words are used figuratively (i.e. not literally) with the ONE EXCEPTION of

A 'legacy' (l. 7)
B 'ravages' (l. 11)
C 'blighted' (l. 20)
D 'riddled' (l. 30)
E 'mar' (l. 34)

8   We must deduce from lines 20–33 that in the most seriously affected districts, patches of derelict land are

A especially ugly
B a large part of the total area
C out-of-date
D randomly scattered
E examples of ribbon development

9   Which of the following comments on metaphors or comparisons is NOT true?

A in l. 30 the holes in the face of the earth are compared to those in a sieve
B in l. 30 the holes made by subsidence are compared to those made by smallpox
C in l. 31 the holes made in the ground by quarrying are compared to wounds made by a sword
D in l. 31 disused machinery is compared to waste paper dropped in a beauty spot
E in l. 35 dust and fumes are compared to acid which eats away cloth

10   'Invites the squatter's shack' (l. 41) means that the
      existence of all this ugliness

      A persuades vandals to destroy other people's
        wooden buildings
      B encourages people to build ramshackle huts on
        derelict land
      C forces people to live in inadequate houses
      D compels people to retain buildings that were
        better demolished
      E makes it legal for squatters to build on unclaimed
        land

11   In explaining the evil effects of dereliction (lines 34–47)
      this writer considers the worst to be that

      A the atmosphere becomes polluted
      B children's lives are endangered as they play
      C rats and mice are encouraged
      D people cease to appreciate beauty
      E vandals and squatters move on to the derelict land

12   'Glib' (l. 48) means

      A talkative
      B flattering
      C insincere
      D thoughtless
      E illogical

13   A 'cliché' (l. 48) means a literary phrase that is

      A used by too many people
      B a round generalisation
      C a poor excuse
      D not genuine or thoughtful
      E out-of-date and no longer appropriate

14   'Where there's muck, there's money' (l. 48) is an
      argument which this article

      A accepts
      B modifies
      C rejects
      D inherits
      E ridicules

15 'Eradicated' (l. 43) means

    A torn up by the roots
    B got rid of completely
    C alleviated slightly
    D improved quickly
    E changed drastically

16 'Abate' (l. 52) means

    A remove
    B cure
    C reduce
    D minimise
    E weaken

17 'Sullies' (l. 54) means

    A tarnishes
    B disfigures
    C defiles
    D disgraces
    E makes unproductive

18 The sentence 'Some of the land . . . it' (l. 55) presents an argument which the article

    A rejects as too costly
    B accepts as counterbalancing serious evils
    C welcomes but considers unimportant
    D emphasises as a main argument
    E is subtly satirising

19 Land that is 'visually redeemed' (ll. 88 and 97) will be

    A obviously reclaimed
    B made more beautiful to look at
    C made nearly as useful as before
    D hidden from view
    E restored to its former purpose

20 This article makes the following proposals for land in Category A(ii) (lines 78–85)

    i holes should not be filled in at once

    ii they should be later used as places to tip rubbish

    iii later they should be sites for houses or playing fields

    iv they should be used for tipping rubbish, or else good farming land would be used instead

    v temporary steps should be taken to hide the worst ugliness

    A i, ii and iii

    B i, iii and v

    C ii, iv and v

    D i, ii, iii and v

    E all of them

21 In the case of land in category A (lines 63–85) it is essential that we

    A use it for building and other purposes in preference to using good farm land

    B keep it as open land near towns

    C plant it with grass and trees

    D restore it to use as permanent farmland

    E avoid spending too much money on it

22 The net addition (l. 91) refers to acres

    A which have been made derelict but rapidly reclaimed

    B whose area has not been over-estimated

    C that have recently been made derelict and have not been reclaimed

    D including all types of dereliction

    E whose area has been estimated but not accurately measured

23 The writer uses the phrase 'cosmetic titivation' (l. 98) to refer to a process that he

    A recommends

    B disapproves of

    C thinks inadequate

D makes fun of

E despises

24 'Reclamation' (l. 100) describes a programme of

    A restoring the land to some kind of use

    B removing ugly ruins of industrial buildings

    C selling the land at a profit

    D bringing the land back into cultivation

    E using the land for building

25 Which ONE of the following statements is NOT true?

    A sites labelled A(i) are the ones most suitable for building

    B sites labelled A(i) should be built on in preference to agricultural land near farms

    C sites labelled A(ii) should also be built on in the near future

    D sites labelled B are too remote to be sites for factories or houses

    E sites labelled C form about a quarter of the new mines and quarries being developed today

26 Land that is 'economically ripe for urban development' (l. 104) would

    A be useful as sites for building or extending towns

    B be useful in a variety of ways

    C be profitable to use for building

    D form a useful reserve of land

    E be a site for prosperous industries

2

Luck and the disunity of his opponents will account for much of Hitler's success—as it will for much of Napoleon's—but not for all. He began with few advantages, a man without a name and without support other than that which he acquired for himself, not even a citizen of the country he   5 aspired to rule. To achieve what he did, Hitler needed—and possessed—talents out of the ordinary which in sum amounted to political genius, however evil in its fruits.

His abilities were his mastery of the irrational factors in politics, his insight into the weaknesses of his opponents,   10

his gift for simplification, his sense of timing, his willingness
to take risks. An opportunist entirely without principle, he
showed considerable consistency and an astonishing power of
will in pursuing his aims. Cynical and calculating in the
exploitation of his histrionic gifts, he retained an unshaken   15
belief in his historic role and in himself as a creature of
destiny.

The fact that his career ended in failure, and that his
defeat was pre-eminently due to his own mistakes, does not
by itself detract from Hitler's claim to greatness. The flaw   20
lies deeper. For these remarkable powers were combined
with an ugly and strident egotism, a moral and intellectual
cretinism. The passions which ruled Hitler's mind were
ignoble: hatred, resentment, the lust to dominate, and,
where he could not dominate, to destroy. His career did not   25
exalt but debased the human condition, and his twelve
years' dictatorship was barren of all ideas save one—the
further extension of his own power and that of the nation
with which he identified himself. Even power he conceived
of in the crudest terms: an endless vista of military roads,   30
S.S. garrisons, and concentration camps to sustain the rule of
the Aryan 'master race' over the degraded subject peoples of
his new empire in the east.

The great revolutions of the past, whatever their ultimate
fate, have been identified with the release of certain powerful   35
ideas: individual conscience, liberty, equality, national
freedom, social justice. National Socialism produced
nothing. Hitler constantly exalted force over the power of
ideas and delighted to prove that men were governed by
cupidity, fear, and their baser passions. The sole theme of   40
the Nazi revolution was domination, dressed up as the
doctrine of race, and, failing that, a vindictive
destructiveness. . . .

It is this emptiness, this lack of anything to justify the
suffering he caused, rather than his own monstrous and   45
ungovernable will, which makes Hitler both so repellent and
so barren a figure. Hitler will have his place in history, but
it will be alongside Attila the Hun, the barbarian king who
was surnamed, not 'the Great', but 'the Scourge of God', and
who boasted 'in a saying', Gibbon writes, 'worthy of his   50

ferocious pride, that the grass never grew on the spot where
his horse had stood'.

Objective Questions

1   The first paragraph (lines 1–8) deals chiefly with
  . Hitler's

    A circumstances
    B virtues
    C upbringing
    D abilities
    E ambitions

2   The first paragraph stresses most of all that Hitler

    A was lucky
    B found his opponents divided
    C resembled Napoleon
    D was a brilliant politician
    E pursued evil policies

3   'Account for' (l. 1) means

    A measure the achievement of
    B provide an opportunity for
    C offer a justification of
    D reduce the size of
    E provide an explanation for

4   'Aspired' (l. 6) means

    A longed
    B rose
    C hoped
    D aimed
    E expected

5   The second paragraph

    A emphasises the ideas of the first paragraph
    B attempts to justify Hitler's actions
    C expands the idea of the word 'talents' in l. 7
    D postpones all mention of his limitations
    E ends by introducing the topic of his faults

6 The word in the second paragraph that is most critical of Hitler is

    A 'irrational' (l. 9)
    B 'weakness' (l. 10)
    C 'opportunist' (l. 12)
    D 'cynical' (l. 14)
    E 'histrionic' (l. 15)

7 His mastery of the irrational factors in politics (l. 9) refers to his

    A understanding of people's emotions and motives
    B ability to win devotion from his followers
    C resolve to encourage the prejudice of his supporters
    D refusal to accept the misjudgments of others
    E ability to plan a long way ahead

8 An 'opportunist' (l. 12) is one who prefers to do what is

    A selfish and unprincipled
    B well-timed and appropriate
    C easy in present circumstances
    D in keeping with his theories
    E relevant to his ambitions

9 'Cynical' (l. 14) means believing that

    A confidence in one's destiny will bring success
    B planning ahead is all important
    C luck is decisive in life
    D other people are moved by selfish motives
    E politicians should persist in their aims

10 The third paragraph does NOT

    A reverse the main argument in opposition to the first two paragraphs
    B agree with the ideas of the fourth and fifth paragraphs
    C make it clear that the author is very critical of Hitler
    D act as a bridge between the ideas of the second and fourth paragraphs

    E contradict completely the ideas of the first para-
       graph

11 'Detract from' (l. 20) means

    A reduce
    B contradict
    C disallow
    D question
    E expose

12 'Strident' (l. 22) means

    A repellent
    B shrill
    C grating
    D noisy
    E harsh

13 'Egotism' (l. 22) means

    A cruelty
    B negativeness
    C selfishness
    D overconfidence
    E obstinacy

14 Which ONE of the following comments on metaphors is
    NOT true?

    A in l. 20 Hitler's negativeness is compared to a
       crack in a piece of crockery
    B in l. 23 Hitler's morality and intellect are com-
       pared to the brain of a deformed idiot
    C in l. 27 his dictatorship which produced no
       positive idea is compared to land which produces
       no crops
    D in l. 30 his ambitious plans for military roads are
       compared to an illusion
    E in l. 35 the ideas spread by revolutions are com-
       pared to prisoners set free from prison

15 The statement that Hitler 'delighted to prove that men were governed by cupidity, fear and their baser passions' (lines 39–40) echoes the idea of the following word in the previous paragraph

    A 'mastery'
    B 'irrational'
    C 'opportunist'
    D 'cynical'
    E 'histrionic'

16 A 'destructiveness' that is 'vindictive' (l. 42) is based on

    A anger
    B revenge
    C selfishness
    D racial hatred
    E ideology

17 'National Socialism produced nothing' (l. 37) means that

    A Hitler accused the Socialists of achieving nothing
    B National Socialism made no lasting converts
    C Hitler's movement had no noble aims
    D Hitler's rule did not increase productivity
    E Hitler's career ended in failure

18 This writer argues that Hitler's worst feature was his

    A belief in force
    B racialist ideas
    C lack of positive ideas for improving mankind
    D complete resolve to get his own way
    E negative insistence on revenge

19 This writer compared Hitler to Attila because both were

    A utterly barbaric
    B great in a terrible way
    C grimly resolute
    D negative and destructive
    E callous

20 The main idea of the passage is that Hitler was

    A great although his career ended in failure
    B not great because he had no genuine ideal

    C great if we judge him by his military power
    D not great because his rule did not last
    E not great because his enemies were divided

Other Questions

1 What abilities and successes does this writer concede to Hitler?
2 Why does Hitler not deserve to be classed as *great*?
3 In what ways did he resemble (1) Napoleon (2) Attila?
4 Explain the following phrases by expressing them in your own words:
    his mastery of the irrational factors in politics (line 9)
    his insight into the weakness of his opponents (l. 10)
    an opportunist entirely without principle (l. 12)
    the exploitation of his histrionic gifts (l. 15)
    belief in his historic role and in himself as a creature of destiny (l. 16)
5 Explain the full meaning in their context of the following words which are used metaphorically:
    fruits (l. 8), role (l. 16), flaw (l. 20), barren (l. 27), scourge (l. 49)
6 In what sense, and in whose eyes, were the subject peoples of the east *degraded* (l. 32)?

TEST 12

Section I TOPICS FOR COMPOSITION

A Write a composition of about 450 words on one of the following subjects:

    1 A dealer buys and sells an article on the same day. Describe the two transactions

    2 The persistent disadvantages of having been born a female

    3 Describe a district or country you have visited or read about which is quite different from the place where you live

    4 What are your views on gambling?

    5 Write a story, real or fictitious, illustrating the value of perseverance in spite of difficulties or setbacks

B Write about 200 words on one of the following:

    1 A letter to a neighbour apologising for damage you have accidentally caused to his property, explaining the circumstances in which the damage was done

    2 Describe clearly one of the following and explain how it works or how it is used:

        a hair-drier, a vacuum cleaner, an electric food-mixer, an electric drill, a motor mower

    3 Write out the instructions which you as leader would give to the members of one of the following:

        (i) a school party going abroad for the first time

        (ii) a party of young people going on an adventure holiday of some kind in this country

    4 Write a report of a serious traffic hold-up, giving clearly its causes, extent, and effects

Section II SUMMARY AND COMPREHENSION

1 Read the following extract from the play *Antigone* by Jean Anouilh and answer the questions on it.

(After the death of Oedipus, king of Thebes, his two sons, Eteocles and Polynices, fought for the throne and killed each other. Creon, their uncle, now king, having sided with Eteocles, decrees that he be given full religious burial, but that Polynices should be left

unburied without any religious rites. Antigone, daughter of 5
Oedipus, is determined to perform this last service for her brother,
although she knows that it is almost certain death to disobey
Creon's orders. At night she scatters earth on Polynices' dead
body, is arrested, and brought before Creon. Antigone is a symbol
of those who put their duty to their family before their duty to 10
their ruler and their state.)

Creon: Why did you try to bury your brother?

Antigone: I owed it to him.

Creon: I had forbidden it.

Antigone: I owed it to him. Those who are not buried wander 15
eternally and find no rest. If my brother were alive, and he
came home weary after a long day's hunting, I should
kneel down and unlace his boots, I should fetch him food
and drink, I should see that his bed was ready for him.
Polynices is home from the hunt. I owe it to him to unlock 20
the house of the dead in which my father and my mother
are waiting to welcome him. Polynices has earned his rest.

Creon: Polynices was a rebel and a traitor, and you know it.

Antigone: He was my brother.

Creon: You heard my edict. It was proclaimed throughout 25
Thebes. You read my edict. It was posted up on the city
walls.

Antigone: Of course I did.

Creon: You knew the punishment I decreed for any person
who attempted to give him burial. 30

Antigone: Yes, I knew the punishment.

Creon: Did you by any chance act on the assumption that a
daughter of Oedipus, a daughter of Oedipus' stubborn
pride, was above the law?

Antigone: No, I did not act on that assumption. 35

Creon: Because if you had acted on that assumption Antigone,
you would have been deeply wrong. Nobody has a more
sacred obligation to obey the law than those who make
the law. You are a daughter of law-makers, a daughter of
kings, Antigone. You must obey the law. 40

Antigone: Had I been a scullery maid, washing my dishes
when that law was read aloud to me, I should have
scrubbed the greasy water from my arms and gone out in
my apron to bury my brother.

Creon: What nonsense! If you had been a scullery maid, there 45
would have been no doubt in your mind about the serious-
ness of that edict. You would have known that it meant
death; and you would have been satisfied to weep for your
brother in your kitchen. But you! You thought that
because you come of the royal line, because you were my 50
niece and were going to marry my son, I shouldn't dare
to have you killed.

Antigone: You are mistaken. Quite the contrary. I never
doubted for an instant that you would have me put to
death. 55

Creon: Tell me, Antigone, do you believe all that flummery
about religious burial? Do you really believe that a so-
called shade of your brother is condemned to wander
for ever homeless if a little earth is not flung on his
corpse to the accompaniment of some priestly abracadabra? 60
Have you ever listened to the priests of Thebes when
they were mumbling their formula? Have you ever
watched those dreary bureaucrats while they were preparing the dead for burial—skipping half the gestures
required by the ritual, swallowing half their words, 65
hustling the dead into their graves out of fear that they
might be late for lunch?

Antigone: Yes, I have seen all that.

Creon: And did you never say to yourself as you watched
them, that if someone you really loved lay dead under the 70
shuffling, mumbling ministrations of the priests, you
would scream aloud and beg the priests to leave the dead
in peace?

Antigone: Yes, I've thought of all that.

Creon: And you still insist upon being put to death—merely 75
because I refuse to let your brother go out with that
grotesque passport; because I refuse his body the wretched
consolation of that mass-production jibber-jabber, which
you would have been the first to be embarrassed by if I
had allowed it. The whole thing is absurd! 80

Antigone: Yes, it's absurd.

Creon: Then why, Antigone, why? For whose sake? For the
sake of them that believe in it? To raise them against me?

Antigone: No.

Creon: For whom then if not for them and not for Polynices   85
either?

Antigone: For nobody. For myself.

Creon: You must want very much to die. You look like a
trapped animal.

Antigone: Stop feeling sorry for me. Do as I do. Do your job.   90
But if you are a human being, do it quickly. That is all I ask
of you. I'm not going to be able to hold out for ever.

Creon: I want to save you, Antigone.

Antigone: You are the king, and you are all-powerful. But
that you cannot do.   95

Creon: You think not?

Antigone: Neither save me nor stop me.

Creon: Prideful Antigone!

Antigone: Only this you can do: have me put to death.

Creon: Have you tortured, perhaps?   100

Antigone: Why would you do that? To see me cry? To hear
me beg for mercy? Or swear whatever you wish, and then
begin over again?

Creon: You listen to me. You have cast me for the villain in
this little play of yours, and yourself for the heroine. And   105
you know it, you damned little mischief-maker! But don't
you drive me too far! If I were one of your preposterous
little tyrants that Greece is full of, you would be lying in a
ditch this minute with your tongue pulled out and your
body drawn and quartered. But you can see something in   110
my face that makes me hesitate to send for the guards
and turn you over to them. Instead, I let you go on arguing;
and you taunt me, you take the offensive. What are you
driving at, you she-devil?

Antigone: Let me go. You are hurting my arm.   115

Creon: I will not let you go.

Antigone: Oh!

Creon: I was a fool to waste words. I should have done
this from the beginning. I may be your uncle—but we are
not a particularly affectionate family. Are we, eh? Are we?   120
What fun for you, eh? To be able to spit in the face of a
king who has all the power in the world; a man who has
done his own killing in his day; who has killed people just
as pitiable as you are—and who is still soft enough to go to

all this trouble to keep you from being killed. 12

Antigone: Now you are squeezing my arm too tightly. It doesn't hurt any more.

Creon: I shall save you yet. God knows, I have things enough to do today without wasting my time on an insect like you. There's plenty to do, I assure you, when you've 13 just put down a revolution. But urgent things can wait. I am not going to let politics be the cause of your death. For it is a fact that this whole business is nothing but politics: the mournful shade of Polynices, the decomposing corpse, the sentimental weeping and the hysteria that 13 you mistake for heroism—nothing but politics.

Look here. I may not be soft, but I'm fastidious, I like things clean, ship-shape, well scrubbed. Don't think that I am not just as offended as you are by the thought of that meat rotting in the sun. In the evening, when the breeze 14 comes in off the sea, you can smell it in the palace, and it nauseates me. But I refuse even to shut my window. It's vile; and I can tell you what I wouldn't tell anybody else: it's stupid, monstrously stupid. But the people of Thebes have got to have their noses rubbed into it a 14 little longer. My God! If it was up to me, I should have had them bury your brother long ago as a mere matter of public hygiene. I admit that what I am doing is childish. But if the feather-headed rabble I govern are to understand what's what, that stench has got to fill the town for a 15 month!

Antigone: You are a loathsome man!

Creon: I agree. My trade forces me to be. We could argue whether I ought or ought not to follow my trade; but once I take on the job, I must do it properly. 15

Antigone: Why do you do it at all?

Creon: My dear, I woke up one morning and found myself King of Thebes. God knows, there were other things I loved in life more than power.

Antigone: Then you should have said no. 16

Creon: Yes, I could have done that. Only, I felt that it would have been cowardly. I should have been like a workman who turns down a job that has to be done. So I said yes.

Antigone: So much the worse for you, then. I didn't say yes.   165
I can say no to anything I think vile, and I don't have to
count the cost. But because you said yes, all that you can
do, for all your crown and trappings, and your guards—all
that you can do is to have me killed.

Creon: Listen to me.   170

Antigone: If I want to. I don't have to listen to you if I don't
want to. You've said your *yes*. There is nothing more you
can tell me that I don't know. You stand there, drinking
in my words. Why is it that you don't call your guards?
I'll tell you why. You want to hear me out to the end;   175
that's why.

Creon: You amuse me.

Antigone: Oh, no, I don't. I frighten you. That is why you
talk about saving me. Everything would be so much easier
if you had a docile, tongue-tied little Antigone living in the   180
palace. I'll tell you something, Uncle Creon: I'll give you
back one of your own words. You are too fastidious to
make a good tyrant. But you are going to have to put me
to death today, and you know it. And that's what
frightens you. God! Is there anything uglier than a   185
frightened man!

Creon: Very well, I am afraid, then. Does that satisfy you?
I am afraid that if you insist upon it, I shall have to have
you killed. And I don't want to.

Antigone: I don't have to do things that I think are wrong.   190
If it comes to that, you didn't really want to leave my
brother's body unburied, did you? Say it! Admit that you
didn't.

Creon: I have said it already.

Antigone: But you did it just the same. And now, though   195
you don't want to do it, you are going to have me killed.
And you call that being a king!

Creon: Yes, I call that being a king.

Antigone: Poor Creon! My nails are broken, my fingers are
bleeding, my arms are covered with the welts left by the   200
paws of your guards—but I am a queen!

Creon: Then why not have pity on me, and live? Isn't your
brother's corpse, rotting there under my windows,
payment enough for peace and order in Thebes? My son

loves you. Don't make me add your life to the payment. 20
I've paid enough.
Antigone: No, Creon! You said yes, and made yourself king.
Now you will never stop paying.

(a) In the first part of this dialogue, what reasons does Antigone give for trying to bury her brother?
(b) For what reasons, according to Creon, had Antigone dared to defy his edict? How does he argue against these reasons?
(c) From Creon's speech (lines 56 to 67), what do you gather is his attitude to Greek burial rites? Quote and comment on words and phrases which especially convey this attitude.
(d) In line 80, Creon says 'The whole thing is absurd.' What effect on the audience in a theatre has Antigone's answer 'Yes, it's absurd'?
(e) Explain in your own words the arguments used by Creon in the speech beginning 'You listen to me . . .' (lines 104 to 114).
(f) Show that you know the meaning of the italicised words is in the following:
    (i) I'm not going *to be able to hold out for ever* (line 92)
    (ii) You have *cast me for the villain in this little play of yours* (l. 104)
    (iii) you *taunt* me, you *take the offensive* (l. 113)
    (iv) the people of Thebes have got *to have their noses rubbed in it* a little longer (l. 145)
    (v) if you had a *docile, tongue-tied* little Antigone (l. 180)
(g) What do you learn from this extract of Creon's character as shown by his attitude (i) to his people (ii) to Antigone?
(h) What do you learn of Antigone from this extract?
(i) Do you admire her more than Creon? Give reasons for your answer.
(j) In a few sentences indicate any resemblances you can see between Creon and modern rulers or politicians.
(k) Would you agree that Creon and Antigone begin by speaking about their religion like superstitious Ancient Greeks and end by speaking about it like sceptical people of today? Give your reasons briefly for agreeing or disagreeing with this view.

Objective Questions

Answer each of the following questions by writing down the letter that stands for the best answer.

1 Which of the following remarks show that Antigone accepts traditional Greek ideas about religion and death more fully than Creon does?

  i Those who are not buried wander eternally and find no rest
  ii I owe it to him to unlock the house of the dead
  iii My father and mother are waiting to welcome him
  iv Had I been a scullery maid . . . I should have gone out in my apron to bury my brother
  v Have you ever listened to the priests of Thebes when they were mumbling their formula?

  A i, ii, iii, and iv
  B i, iii, iv, and v
  C i, ii, iv, and v
  D ii, iii, iv, and v
  E all of them

2 Which of the following statements about metaphors or comparisons is NOT true?

  A l. 17 compares a man who is dead and needs a religious burial to one who has been hunting and needs a welcome home
  B ll. 33–4 compare a person too rich, powerful or noble to bother to keep the law to one who is physically raised above something he or she can ignore
  C ll. 63–7 compare the priests who put no conviction into their burial services to officials or clerks who have no interest in their job
  D ll. 76–7 compare a burial service, an entry to another life, to a passport, an entry to another country
  E ll. 92–3 compare Antigone, continuing to reject Creon's pleas, to a container continuing to hold a liquid

3 The speech of Antigone (l. 15) does NOT

    A unconsciously assume that men are more important than women

    B use 'home from the hunt' as a metaphor to represent death

    C regard a proper burial of a dead man's body as essential to the future of his soul

    D show respect for her dead brother

    E emphatically justify her brother's defiance of Creon

4 All the following remarks remind us that Creon is a king with the ONE EXCEPTION of

    A I had forbidden it (l. 14)

    B You heard my edict. It was proclaimed throughout Thebes (l. 25)

    C You knew the punishment I decreed for any person who attempted to give him burial (l. 29)

    D Nobody has a more sacred obligation to obey the law than those who make the law (l. 37)

    E Do you really believe that a so-called shade of your brother is condemned to wander for ever homeless if a little earth is not flung on his corpse? (l. 57)

5 Which of the following statements are true of lines 36–52?

    i Creon accuses Antigone of thinking that a king's daughter does not need to keep the law

    ii Antigone claims this right as belonging to her royal rank

    iii Creon says that members of a royal family must keep the law more carefully than anyone else

    iv Creon is quite sure that the daughter of an ordinary citizen would obey his decree and not bury her brother in defiance of it

    v Creon is reluctant to kill the woman who is betrothed to marry his son

    A i, ii, and iii

    B i, iii, and iv

    C i, ii, and iv

D i, iii, and v
E all of them

6 Creon insists that a scullery maid, unlike Antigone,
   would

A have been busy doing housework when she heard
   of the king's edict
B have been afraid of execution if she disobeyed it
C have buried her brother despite Creon's edict
D NOT have hoped to obtain a special pardon
E have preferred to leave the house she was in

7 In l. 56 Creon changes the basis of his argument
   because he now

A realises that Antigone expects to be executed
B turns his back on his former acceptance of
   traditional religion
C tries to persuade Antigone to take religion
   seriously
D wonders how his son will react
E assumes that Antigone has not watched the
   priests' activities very closely

8 The extract from the play first becomes more modern
   and sceptical of Greek religion at the point when

A Creon uses the word 'flummery'
B Creon refers to the priests as 'dreary bureaucrats'
C Creon uses the phrase 'priestly abracadabra'
D Creon uses the phrase 'grotesque passport'
E Antigone admits, 'It's absurd'

9 Which of the following possible motives for Antigone
   does Creon suggest?

A that members of a royal family need not keep the
   law
B that Creon would never execute his son's fiancée
C that she intends to provoke a rebellion
D that she wants to find a way of committing suicide
E that she puts her duty to her family before her duty
   to the state

G

10 Antigone argues that Creon's decision to have her executed

    A is one which he could easily reverse
    B is the act of a tyrant who overvalues power
    C follows inevitably from his acceptance of kingly power
    D is the result of a series of events quite independent of his actions
    E shows that he is not really fond of his son

11 Which of the following arguments does Creon make in the speech beginning 'You listen to me' (l. 104)?

    i Antigone has twisted the truth so that *he* becomes like a villain in a play
    ii If he were as bad as she paints him, he would have killed her already
    iii She recognises the pity and weakness in him that prevent him from being a real tyrant
    iv Instead of his killing her at once, she is provoking him
    v He does not understand her motives

    A i, ii, and iii
    B i, ii, iii, and iv
    C i, ii, iv, and v
    D i, iii, iv, and v
    E all of them

12 Creon argues in the speech beginning 'I was a fool' (l. 118) that

    A he does not keep Antigone's brother unburied for religious reasons
    B he ought to have used force against her earlier
    C he can withstand unconcernedly the presence of her brother's rotting corpse
    D he has decided to bury her brother at once
    E his actions are not dictated by the need to impress his subjects

13 'Fastidious' (l. 137) means

    A hard to please

    B overcautious
    C sensitive
    D squeamish
    E discriminating

14 'Docile' (l. 180) means

    A subservient
    B timid
    C tamely obedient
    D taciturn   ·
    E quietly shy

15 The deduction to be made most directly from this interview is that

    A one's duty to one's family should come before one's duty to the state
    B in a political question there is often both right and wrong on both sides
    C those who accept power must afterwards act from necessity, not choice
    D capital punishment is never justifiable
    E one should never carry any course of action to extremes

2 Read the following passage, which describes Bondi, a beach in Sydney (Australia), and then answer the questions on it.

    Bondi, this afternoon, at last as postcards show it. A dazzling arc of sand plunging to two house-hung headlands, the whiteness almost obliterated by brown flesh. The breakers come in long and foaming, arching up out of a sulky, silken sea. The sky blue, devoid of cloud, and coloured   5
umbrellas speckling the beach. Bondi is brazen, vulgar, vivid and marvellous in its contrasts. The open Pacific, sea of explorers, for whom this coast was the mirage realised, stirs at the feet of a packed half-moon of settlers, airing bodies and minds, craving the ocean.   10
    At Bondi the timid majority wallow and splash safely between flags of safety, whistled out of rips and undertows by pedagogic beach inspectors. But these are, as it were, only

the necessary chorus of Greek drama, affording the crowd-
movement, violent but circumscribed, against which the   15
heroes and heroines, the surfers, perform their exploits.

For, far beyond the noisy huddle cavorting in the shallows,
the surfers swim out to the first line of breakers, perhaps
three hundred yards from the shore. That initial swim,
through waves half a house high, is the essential prologue.   20
To reach the point of departure for the surf-journey, that
final green, remorseless and motionless flight to rest, requires
that you are not merely an excellent swimmer, but a strong,
enduring one.

Around where the impulse of the ocean begins to shape   25
itself visibly, the surfers turn, creating an imaginary, calcu-
lated line. Beyond them, the shark-boat, manned by half a
dozen capped and mahogany oarsmen, idles on the last strip
of patient sea. The heads of the surfers bob over several
ignored undulations. Then, expert eyes having read and   30
approved a particular wave's physique as skilfully as breeders
size up the prowess of horses, the line strikes out for the
shore, making a score of frenzied strokes before the wave
arches. Someone may lose the impetus, having estimated
wrongly, and have to turn back. The others, acquiring one   35
by one the final motive force of the Pacific airs, stop swimming: and, the fifteen-foot wave suspended like a banner
from their breasts, they take the current as motionlessly as
the albatross, the sea hollowing under them, a hollow into
which they look far down, and, doing no more than lean   40
on their springs of foam, glide proudly in. This last surge up
the beach is compounded of the elements of flight and diving
—man becoming a sea-bird.

The essential art of surfing is timing, instinct developed by
knowledge of when to turn, of when to start swimming, of   45
friendly and cruel waves. There are kinds of seas, species of
waves and current, the distinguishing of which requires years
of apprenticeship. The technique is simple in expression,
elaborate in its subtle harnessing of the body to racing air.
For, of course, it is only the air behind the wave, not the   50
water itself, that moves. And it is propelled by the air, and
supported by the wave, that the surfer comes in to his long,
clean climax.

The bad wave, which the novice fails usually to discern, is the 'dumper', an ugly curling wave that, not coming to a   55
perceptible head, throws the swimmer under it and batters him repeatedly. Being 'dumped' is as necessary a part of the surfer's experience as being thrown is of the jockey's.

Surfing, as we saw this afternoon at Bondi, when teams from the neighbouring clubs of Bronte, Maroubra, and   60
Manly competed with Bondi in a surf carnival, has several forms of expression. Boards are used, beautiful to watch when the rider stands up straight, arched against sea and sky, appearing to be motionless, but in fact readjusting his balance with neat dancer's steps. In carnivals, boat teams race out to   65
coloured floats on the water, rowing their boats in on the surf against one another and beaching them. The afternoon begins with the parade, when the pageantry of life-saving, which is the graver corollary to use of the surf, is demonstrated in a march-past. The teams, wearing costumes and bathing   70
caps striped with club colours, parade round a marked area of beach, carrying their equipment of belts and reels, and stepping out high and robustly on the sand. There is, to the casual eye, an element of absurdity about this solemn-faced stamping in antique costumes; but in fact, once one has got   75
used to the startling sight of so many men the size and colour of wardrobes, all marching in rhythmic procession, one takes the presence of the uniformed life-saver on the beach for granted. Which is what should not be done, for these men, who pay 10s. 6d a year for the privilege of risking their   80
lives, as well as devoting hundreds of hours to training and practice, on an average rescue over a thousand people a summer.

(a) Suggest four reasons why this author succeeds, or fails, in making you want to see Bondi
(b) Quote a phrase that shows that Bondi was crowded
(c) Why does surfing require hard effort?
(d) What measures are taken to keep bathing safe?
(e) Describe the motions of a surfer as he
    (1) turns towards the shore
    (2) gets very near the shore
(f) Choose two striking metaphors; briefly defend your choice

(g) Comment on three details that make the description vivid
(h) This writer calls Bondi *vulgar* and *marvellous*. How does he
    go on to justify these adjectives?
(i) Why does he admire the life-savers?
(j) Comment on the effectiveness of the description of surfing
    as 'man becoming a sea-bird'.
(k) What does Alan Ross gain or lose in the first paragraph by
    writing some sentences without main verbs?

Objective Questions

1 Which of the following is not a reason why Ross finds
   Bondi attractive?
   A The breakers of the sea sweep majestically in
   B The colours of the sand and the sky are dramatic
   C It is the ideal setting for the drama staged by the
      surfers
   D It is the realisation of the explorers' dreams
   E It illustrates the spaciousness of Australia

2 'obliterated' (l. 3) means

   A covered
   B hidden
   C disguised
   D marred
   E spoiled

3 Which ONE of the following words is used literally and
   not metaphorically?
   A 'arching' (l. 4)
   B 'sulky' (l. 4)
   C 'vulgar' (l. 6)
   D 'mirage' (l. 8)
   E 'half-moon' (l. 9)

4 The beach inspectors (l. 13) are like
   A policemen
   B guards
   C old-maids
   D schoolteachers
   E doctors

5 Which of the following are among the marvellous contrasts of Bondi?

    i the spacious ocean and the packed beach
    ii the timid bathers and heroic surfers
    iii the easy swim out to sea and the dramatic release
    iv the surfers and the life-savers
    v the decorous solemnity of the life-savers' parade and the grim necessity for their work

    A i, ii and iii
    B i, ii and v
    C i, iii and v
    D i, ii and iv
    E all of them

6 'Circumscribed' (l. 15) means

    A surrounded
    B limited
    C vulgar
    D provincial
    E overshadowed

7 Two words very similar in meaning, and repeating the same idea, are

    A violent .... circumscribed (l. 15)
    B noisy .... cavorting (l. 17)
    C initial .... prologue (l. 19 and l. 20)
    D remorseless .... enduring (l. 22 and l. 24)
    E impulse .... patient (l. 25 and l. 29)

8 The swimmers are like the 'necessary chorus of Greek drama' (l. 14) in that they

    A sing like characters in a Greek play
    B play second fiddle to more dramatic people
    C introduce an element of violence
    D are capable of extraordinary exploits
    E obey the orders of others

9 'Initial' (l. 19) means

    A outward
    B magnificent
    C dramatic
    D first
    E difficult

10 For the surfers the swim outwards, away from the shore, is

    A exhausting
    B arduous
    C motionless
    D dramatic
    E marvellous

11 The surfers begin their shoreward journey where the

    A Pacific Ocean becomes impulsive
    B six oarsmen keep watch for sharks
    C waves that ultimately break on the shore begin to form a noticeable line of foam
    D ocean begins to form a seething mass of foam
    E sea waits patiently before beginning its assault on the land

12 As they turn, the surfers

    A swim through a number of waves
    B make individual decisions
    C decide not to let several waves sweep them shoreward
    D change their minds and swim further out
    E break the straightness of their line-up

13 'Remorseless' (l. 22) means lacking

    A colour
    B impatience
    C impetus
    D disturbance
    E mercy

14 The surfers resemble sea-birds because they

    A stay motionless before they descend suddenly

B are buffeted up and down by currents of air
C are moved by the air behind the wave
D move their arms in the way that a bird moves its
   wings
E develop an elaborate, subtle technique

15 A bad wave

A pushes the surfer underwater
B rises to a great height
C forms a prominent line of foam
D takes a long time to reach a climax
E is something that a surfer soon learns to recognise

16 Which of the following qualities does the writer
    admire VERY MUCH in life-savers?

i   they wear old-fashioned costumes
ii   they actually pay out their own money
iii they rescue a considerable number of people
iv   they spend a lot of time in training and practice
v   they are so tall and sunburnt

A i, ii and ii
B ii, iii and iv
C iii, iv and v
D ii, iv and v
E all of them

TEST 13

A Write an essay of about 450 words on one of the following topics:

    1 Visitors—welcome and unwelcome

    2 Write a character study of a famous person whose work you admire

    3 The intelligence of animals

    4 'Youth and Age can never agree.' From your own experience describe your relationships with three older people, and say how far you agree with this statement

    5 Has the motor-car done more good than harm?

    6 Describe a family reunion, explaining the reactions of people who had not met for a long time

    7 Write what is suggested by one of the following:

      (a) The stars
          Eastward were sparkling clear, and in the west
          The orange sky of evening died away.

      (b) Forget six counties overhung with smoke,
          Forget the snorting steam, and piston stroke,
          Forget the spreading of the hideous town:
          Think rather of the pack-horse on the down,
          And dream of London, small, and white, and clean.

      (c) 'Courage' he said, and pointed toward the land,
          'This mounting wave will roll us shoreward soon.'

      (d) I think continually of those who were truly great.

      (e) From scars where kestrels hover,
          The leading looking over
          Into the happy valley,
          Orchard and curving river,
          May turn away to see
          The slow fastidious line
          That disciplines the fell.

      (f) I'm beginning to lose patience
          With my personal relations.

B 1 Your school is to be enlarged. Among possible additions
      are a lecture room equipped with a wide range of
      visual aids or a sixth form common room or an indoor
      swimming pool. Your headmaster or headmistress has
      asked pupils to produce a written statement, putting
      the case for one of these additions
   2 Choose one of the following devices, explain its purpose
      and how it works: an alarm clock, a lawn-mower, an
      electric food-mixer, the starter of a car, a safety razor,
      a sewing-machine, a stapling machine
   3 Describe for the benefit of a foreign visitor the place in
      British life of one of the following:
         The Cup Final, The Boat-race, Boxing Day, Bank
         Holiday Monday, Guy Fawkes Night, St Valentine's
         Day, A Coffee-bar, Woolworths, Pancake Day
   4 J. B. Priestley wrote a series of short essays about things
      he enjoyed, and collected them into a book called *Delight*.
      For instance, his short essay on 'Orchestras creeping in
      to support the Piano' begins:

'I do not care where it happens, whether it is at the Coketown
Hippodrome or the Royal Albert Hall, or who brings it off,
whether it is Billy Binks, the Comedy Entertainer, or Strugg,
the World's Greatest Pianist, but I never fail to get into a
dingle-dangle of delight, with icy-legged spiders racing up
and down my spine, when suddenly and softly the orchestra
creeps in to accompany the piano. You have almost forgotten about orchestras. And suddenly—and oh so softly at
first—there it is, with the strings whispering below the
familiar silver hammering of the piano, then the wood wind
bubbling and chuckling, then the brass assertive and
triumphant, then the drums and cymbals booming and
clashing to a grand finality. Socrates was wiser than I am;
Alexander and Caesar made bigger names for themselves;
and Shakespeare could write much better than I can. But not
one of them ever heard the orchestra come creeping in to
support the piano and never knew my dingle-dangle of
delight.'

      Write a long paragraph in this mood about why you like
      or dislike one of the following: shopping in unlikely
      places, relaxing, looking at old photographs, fountains,

being up early in the morning, reading for fun, going abroad for the first time, bragging

Section II SUMMARY AND COMPREHENSION

1 Read the following newspaper article and then answer the questions that follow it.

Not one woman sits on the Board in the biggest British Companies, although a few are found on the boards of subsidiaries. Among the lower echelons there are, in contrast, plenty. But extend the search either upwards, to regions of general management, or outwards—away from the consuming and towards the manufacturing end of big business— and you no longer need a computer to count them. Fingers will do. 5

Yet outside big business, there are plenty of women in top places—more than enough to refute allegations that they are either uninterested or incapable of holding down jobs calling for the exercise of skill, decision and responsibility. If they can reach the top elsewhere, why not in big business? 'If you really want to get a job in big business, there's really no difficulty in landing a starter,' says one girl, now in consumer research, who came down from university three years ago. The big companies themselves say they are always on the lookout for promising material. For instance, two years ago I.C.I. began to choose women graduates to appear before its central selection panel for commercial jobs—though for many years, of course, others had entered I.C.I. by direct recruitment for particular posts. 10 15 20

If starting prospects for women in big business are good, is there really need to worry about lack of women at the top now? Is it not possible to write off the problem, as did one senior member of a large firm recently, by putting it down to the sheer lack of women candidates in the past? 25

This would be tempting, but for two things, First, women have now worked in big business long enough for their absence from the top to be due to reasons other than scarcity. And second, too many women in junior managerial posts today would agree with the woman marketing 30

manager who says, 'The fact is, I'm at a standstill—they
haven't a notion how to deal with the 30-plus woman. By the
time they make up their minds I'll be hopelessly behind in   35
the race.'

Women complain of prejudice—but this, to a man, is often
nothing more than due acknowledgement of feminine
frailty. Depressing stories about the resounding failures of
women to shoulder responsibility; harrowing stories of the   40
havoc and embarrassment wrought by weeping women:
ludicrous stories of aggressive tigresses; contradictory
stories of maddening activity or complete lassitude—all
such tales have appeared before in other contexts, and are
evidence not so much of the frailty of women as of the   45
uncommon endurance of myth.

The more one hears of women's liabilities, the more one is
driven to conclude that the majority of allegations either
have no foundation in fact, or are mutually exclusive. And
of those that are founded in fact, a staggering number of   50
them are either true also of men, or have masculine counter-
parts.

Marriage as a reason for leaving seems to excite a disproportionate amount of wrath. Too often the departing
woman is made to feel like the parlourmaid sneaking the   55
spoons, on the grounds that she is unlikely to return to
employment again. 'All that training wasted' is the grumble.
True perhaps. But while it may justify the decision not to
employ women at all, it is no excuse for letting them in and
then penalizing them afterwards—which, after all, merely   60
prejudices them against returning to work in later years.

The majority of allegations of unfair discrimination occur
over questions of pay. Most big businesses will declare with
perfect truth that their salary scales do not differentiate
between the sexes; but there are enough authenticated   65
stories of the practice of regularly starting women some
£250 lower than men of exactly similar qualifications to cast
considerable doubt upon the impartiality of big business
salaries and grading policies.

Again, a very common reaction of managers to the   70
importunings of women for more pay is, 'Well, you're doing
quite well *for a woman,* aren't you?' In contrast the recently

resigned executive of one of Britain's largest companies
said bitterly, 'It's not so much the actual pay that got me
down—but when they promoted men over my head who   75
were far less well qualified than I was, well then I decided
it was time to go.'

Misplaced paternalism accounts for a good deal of the
discrimination actually practised. 'No good manager is
going to risk promoting one of his staff to a position where   80
she will be exposed to difficulties,' is how the head of
Unilever's Information Division puts it, adding, 'and a
woman couldn't possibly do my job because of the amount of
work and entertaining I have to do outside the office.'

The extent of prejudice is hotly contested. Because big   85
business is still so unknown to the public and so many of its
procedures shrouded in secrecy, it is sometimes difficult to
judge whether it does practise discrimination against women
on grounds of their sex.

However frustrated a woman may be in her job and   90
however convinced she may be that she is discriminated
against, big business itself still offers a fascinating, varied and
frequently highly remunerative career. Why then do
comparatively few young women offer themselves for it?

(a) Write a summary in 120 words, saying what evidence
there is of unfair lack of promotion for women in business
(b) Using the material in the article as much or as little as you
like, state how you would try to end (or prolong) the situation described in the article
(c) Choose the topic sentence from any paragraph and show
how it sums up the main theme of the paragraph

Objective Questions

1 In business, women have reached

A a few positions *near* the top
B a few positions *at* the top
C much the same number of positions in all branches
D more important positions than in the past
E very few positions anywhere

2 'Lower echelons' (formations of troops in separate
  sections each behind the other) is used in l. 3 as a metaphorical word for

    A armed forces
    B subordinate jobs
    C civil servants connected with the army
    D unskilled workers
    E working classes

3 To 'refute' (l. 10) means to

    A deny
    B cast doubt on
    C support
    D account for
    E disprove

4 The prejudice against giving women the top jobs is
  strongest in appointing

    A managers of subsidiary firms
    B subordinate managers in large firms
    C directors to the most important firms
    D directors to firms concerned with selling products
    E experts to design computers

5 This writer argues that the most illogical and in-
  excusable action of big business is to

    A employ too few women
    B pay unfairly low salaries to women
    C employ too few women to begin with
    D believe myths about weeping women
    E employ women without offering them top jobs

6 'Frailty' (l. 45) means

    A temperament
    B unreliability
    C weepiness
    D weakness
    E feebleness

7 'Resounding' (l. 39) means

    A repeated
    B sensational
    C credible
    D mythical
    E spreading

8 The repetition of the word 'stories' (lines 39–43) is intended to have several effects on the reader, but it is NOT intended to

    A amuse him a little
    B make him think the stories exaggerated
    C suggest that only gullible people spread them
    D imply that there must be an important truth in them
    E imply that these 'stories' are tales of fiction

9 This writer argues that accusations against women in top jobs of (e.g.) being tigresses or bursting into tears are

    A often inconsistent and contradictory
    B rarely believed by men
    C more true of women than of men
    D evidence that women are still the weaker sex
    E signs of prejudice against employing married women

10 Women's 'liabilities' (l. 47) are

    A weaknesses belonging to women
    B women's responsibilities to their families
    C women's unwillingness to shoulder responsibility
    D women's traditional roles
    E women's protests

11 'Disproportionate' (ll. 53–4) means

    A very large in this context
    B larger than the circumstances warrant
    C irrational and exaggerated
    D based on prejudice
    E habitual and traditional

12 To compare a woman leaving her job on marriage to a parlourmaid sneaking the spoons is to suggest that she

A has fundamentally cheated the company
B is untrustworthy
C is demeaning herself by getting married
D is capable of taking her employer's property
E feels ashamed to be getting married

13 When most big businesses are said to declare something
with 'perfect truth' (ll. 63–4) it is suggested that what
they say is
A not really the truth at all
B inexact and inaccurate
C a traditional myth
D a justifiable reason for action
E true to some extent

14 'Authenticated' (l. 65) means
A widely repeated
B often alleged
C commonly believed
D supported by evidence
E cleverly arranged

15 'Importunings' (l. 71) are
A accusations against injustice
B angry protests
C indignant feelings of self-pity
D instinctive reactions
E repeated requests

16 'Paternalism' (l. 78) means
A an irrational prejudice
B excessive protectiveness
C old-fashioned chivalry
D a belief in masculine superiority
E adherence to traditional virtues

17 'Hotly contested' (l. 85) means
A angrily challenged
B bitterly resented
C deeply felt
D firmly denied
E convincingly measured

18 The main argument of the article is that big business
    A is unwilling to appoint able young women
    B is no more hostile to women than are other branches of commerce or industry
    C lets able women climb so high and no higher
    D cannot attract enough able women
    E thinks women unjustified when they complain of prejudice

19 Among the words that this article uses in order to suggest an intense rivalry among the employees of the same big firm are
    A 'echelons' (l. 3) .... 'computer' (l. 7)
    B 'top places' (l. 10)
    C 'starter' (l. 15) ...... 'promising material' (l. 18)
    D 'recruitment' (l. 22) .. 'prospects' (l. 23)
    E 'standstill' (l. 33) .... 'the race' (l. 36)

20 The one of the following words that is used literally, NOT metaphorically, is
    A 'regions' (l. 4)
    B 'end' (l. 6)
    C 'holding down' (l. 11)
    D 'difficulty' (l. 15)
    E 'lookout' (l. 18)

21 Among the real reasons why there are so few women in top jobs is the fact that
    A there was a shortage of women candidates in the past
    B industry does not make full use of able women over thirty years of age
    C women have often been afraid to shoulder responsibility
    D women tend to vary between extremes of action and inaction
    E too much training is wasted when women in important jobs get married

22 'Contexts' (l. 44) means
    A books
    B countries

C quarters
D situations
E places

23 Which of the following words is used literally, NOT
metaphorically?

A race (l. 36)
B shoulder (l. 40)
C embarrassment (l. 41)
D staggering (l. 50)
E shrouded (l. 87)

The Day of The Triffids

[In the book of this name, from which the following extract
is taken, John Wyndham imagines that two disasters simultaneously attack mankind.

A series of lights in the sky blinds all who look at them—so
that the only ones to save their sight are those who were
asleep, or were down a mine, or (like the narrator) were
lying in a hospital with bandaged eyes. At the same time a
sort of huge onion called a triffid learns to walk and to attack
human beings with a poisonous whip. The narrator escapes
from hospital and meets a girl named Josella who can
see; together they try to avoid murderous triffids, blinded
human beings looking for food, and criminals who can see
and intend to use their sight ruthlessly.]

A few yards up the street we came upon a large, shiny
saloon car. It looked the kind of craft that should simply
have purred. But the noise when I started it up sounded
louder in our ears than all the normal traffic of a busy street.
We made our way northward, zigzagging to avoid derelicts   5
and wanderers stricken into immobility in the middle of
the road by the sound of our approach. All the way heads
turned hopefully towards us as we came; and faces fell as we
went past. One building on our route was blazing fiercely,
and a cloud of smoke rose from another fire somewhere   10
along Oxford Street. There were more people about in
Oxford Circus, but we got through them neatly, then passed
the B.B.C., and so north to the carriageway in Regent's Park.

It was a relief to get out of the streets and reach an open
space—and one where there were no unfortunate people   15
wandering and groping. The only moving things we could
see on the broad stretches of grass were two or three little
groups of triffids lurching southwards. Somehow or other
they had contrived to pull up their stakes and were dragging
them along behind them on their chains. I remembered that   20
there were some undocked specimens, a few tethered, but
most of them double-fenced, in an enclosure beside the zoo,
and wondered how they had got out. Josella noticed them, too.

'It's not going to make much difference to them,' she said.

For the rest of the way there was little to delay us. Within   25
a few minutes I was pulling up at the house she pointed out.
We got out of the car, and I pushed open the gate. A short
drive curved round a bed of bushes which hid most of the
house front from the road. As we turned the corner Josella
gave a cry, and ran forward. A figure was lying on the   30
gravel, chest downwards, but with the head turned to show
one side of its face. The first glance at it showed me the
bright red streak across the cheek.

'Stop!' I shouted at her.

There was enough alarm in my voice to check her.   35

I had spotted the triffid now. It was lurking among the
bushes, well within striking range of the sprawled figure.

'Back! Quick!' I said.

Still looking at the man on the ground, she hesitated.

'But I must——' she began, turning towards me. Then she   40
stopped. Her eyes widened, and she screamed.

I whipped round to find a triffid towering only a few feet
behind me.

In one automatic movement I had my hands over my eyes.
I heard the sting whistle as it lashed out at me—but there   45
was no knockout, no agonised burning, even. One's mind
can move like lightning at such a moment: nevertheless, it was
more instinct than reason which sent me leaping at it before
it had time to strike again. I collided with it, overturning it,
and even as I went down with it my hands were on the upper   50
part of its stem, trying to pull off the cup and the sting.
Triffid stems do not snap—but they can be mangled. This
one was mangled thoroughly before I stood up.

Josella was standing in the same spot, transfixed.

'Come here,' I told her. 'There's another in the bushes be-   55
hind you.'

She glanced fearfully over her shoulder, and came.

'But it *hit* you!' she said, incredulously. 'Why aren't you——?'

'I don't know. I ought to be,' I said.

I looked down at the fallen triffid. Suddenly remembering   60
the knives that we'd acquired with quite other enemies in
mind, I used mine to cut off the sting at its base. I examined it.

'That explains it,' I said, pointing to the poison-sacs. 'See,
they're collapsed, exhausted. If they'd been full, or even part
full . . .' I turned a thumb down.   65

I had that, and my acquired resistance to the poison, to
thank. Nevertheless, there was a pale red mark across the
back of my hands and my neck that was itching like the devil.
I rubbed it while I stood looking at the sting.

(a) In about 70 of your own words describe the journey made by
    the narrator and Josella to the house at which they stopped
(b) Explain the meaning of
    (i) wanderers stricken into immobility (l. 6)
    (ii) it was more instinct than reason (ll. 47–8)
(c) What does the phrase 'wandering and groping' (l. 16)
    convey to you?
(d) What is the effect of the words 'lurching' (l. 18), 'lurking'
    (l. 36), and 'sprawled' (l. 37)?
(e) What difference is intended between 'snap' and 'mangled'
    (l. 52)?
(f) Give the meaning in the passage of the words
    purred (l. 3), transfixed (l. 54), incredulously (l. 58),
    tethered (l. 21)
(g) What did the narrator imply by 'I turned a thumb down . . .'
    (l. 65)?
(h) To what two factors did he attribute his escape from serious
    injury?
(i) Discuss whether the two main characters in this incident
    appear selfish
(j) Which details in the story make it easy to believe?
(k) To what extent does this passage have the qualities that
    you expect from science fiction?

TEST 14

Section I TOPICS FOR COMPOSITION

A Write an essay of about 450 words on one of the following
topics:

1 My first impressions of Hull (or some other town or
village that you care to choose)
2 Childhood recollections
3 A family outing
4 Hooliganism at football matches. (What form does it
take? Why does it occur? How would you prevent it?)
5 You are a nurse or a miner or a steel-worker or a
member of the police force. Last night you worked from
10 p.m. to 6 a.m., with a break for a meal. Write an
account of how you spent the night. You may include,
if you wish, an account of your journeys from home to
work and from work back home
6 Write a narrative that begins: 'It was only recently that
I noticed it, that I was slowly being pushed out of
our gang of friends.'
7 Write a story or a description or an essay suggested by
the picture facing p. 129.

B Write about 250 words on one of the following:
1 Write one of the following letters, giving a suitable
layout, and inventing names and addresses:
   (a) You are on holiday at a place which you think
   that your young aunt and uncle would enjoy.
   Write recommending the place to them
   (b) Six months ago you bought a watch but neglected
   to return the card with details of the purchase
   which would make the year's guarantee effective.
   The watch has now broken down. Write, asking
   the manufacturers if they could still help you

2 Describe the steps you would take to carry out *one* of
the following good resolutions:
   (a) to make a newly arrived immigrant boy or girl
   feel at home in your neighbourhood
   (b) to provide suitable activities for children (of any

age range you choose to specify) at a holiday play centre

3 Explain how to do *one* of the following well. Assume that your reader has tried to do but it is not as good at it as you are:

  (a) grow any specific flower that you care to choose
  (b) wash and polish a car
  (c) look after a friend's dog for a fortnight
  (d) cook your father's favourite pudding
  (e) identify any wind instrument that you care to choose

Section II SUMMARY AND COMPREHENSION

1 Read the following passage and then answer the questions on it.

The English are avid readers of newspapers. No other country in the world has such a massive daily diet of the printed word. That serious, sometimes justified, criticisms can be made of some newspapers in no way alters the fact that they are read in their millions. They are accused of 5 irresponsibility, distortion, political bias, frivolity, sensationalism; of vulgarly and immorally debasing noble values and of prying into private lives—but they are read with relish.

Many of the strictures on the press apply only to a few 10 newspapers; yet the mud clings to all. Criticisms are made against the press when, in reality, the critic means a specific journalist or newspaper. I would suggest that such a nebulous concept as 'The Press' gets in the way of serious discussion. In blaming or praising, it would be better to name the paper 15 or papers under discussion. 'The Press' is an umbrella term covering a wide variety of quite different products. What might be true of the *Daily Sketch* might not be true of *The Times* and *The Guardian;* what might be true of the *News of the World* might not be true of the *Observer.* All that is good, 20 however, is not the exclusive preserve of the 'Quality' Press; the 'Popular' Press does not have a monopoly of all that is bad.

Comparing different papers over a period of time would give pupils some criteria with which to judge the quality and objectivity of the paper they read regularly. It would enable them to distinguish between fact and opinion, between good writing and slipshod, cliché-ridden work. It would lead to a healthy, informed criticism of their daily reading matter. It could change their reading habits. Most school children have much easier access to newspapers than any other form of literature. Newspapers can be used as a stepping-stone to literacy, but only if the pupils have been trained to distinguish the good from the bad, and have been made aware of the numerous techniques used either to inform or to mislead, to provoke thought or stifle it, to evoke real emotion or ersatz emotion.

A newspaper has many functions. One—and only a fool would deny it—is that it must sell, at the right place at the right time. There is nothing ignoble about this: it must pay its way or disappear. To a large extent it has to give its readers what they want.

In his book *Dangerous Estate,* Francis Williams—now Lord Williams—had this to say: 'They [newspapers] hold a mirror to society, and—appalled and fascinated by what the mirror shows—there are many who would like to cut off the hand that holds it.' Too often newspapers are blamed for the ailments of society: after all, people who are offended by the 'Popular' Press can always stop buying the offending paper. That millions of people persist in their reading habits would suggest that they believe they are getting their money's worth; a very real demand is being satisfied.

This, however, is a simplification of the situation. In his book *Uses of Literacy,* Richard Hoggart suggested that people are not being given what they really want. He argued that many newspapers blunt the natural appetite for the real facts. 'The mass-produced bad makes it harder for the good to be recognized', he wrote. His suggestion was this: constantly fed on trivialities, half-truths and gossip, the great reading public is becoming incapable of wanting anything better. And—most important in a democracy— they are not in a position to evaluate real facts and take real decisions because they are never in possession of the relevant

information. There is some truth in this. But there are
newspapers to which it does not apply.

Journalists argue over the functions of a newspaper. I   65
can only offer you my idea of what a provincial paper should
be and should do. Its purpose is not only to present and
project the news objectively and imaginatively, but to help
its readers to express themselves more effectively, canalizing
their aspirations, making more articulate their demands.   70
A newspaper should reflect the community it serves—warts
and all. When the mirror it holds to society reveals neglect,
injustice, inhumanity, ignorance or complacency, the mirror
should not be clouded but polished, so that these things can
be eradicated rather than ignored. And the newspaper   75
should help to eradicate them. It would be pretentious to
think that a local paper (or even a national) can change the
course of world affairs—but at the local level it can exert
influence, it can probe, it can help to get things done. Though,
of necessity, it must concentrate on local affairs it should also   80
try to broaden its readers' horizons, discarding the parish-
pump mentality. In its columns its readers should be encouraged to express their opinions, their fears, their hopes—
and, just as important, air their grievances. In these days of
the big battalions, the individual's voice should not be   85
stifled; the local newspaper should provide the individual
with a platform. In short, readers should be encouraged to
participate in the newspaper. The paper should become
part of their lives, and, as such, its contribution to the
community can be that much greater. A citizen with a   90
grievance can always write to his local paper. If the newspaper is doing its job properly, that grievance will be
investigated—and the paper will help to put it right.

I have dwelt at length on this subject because there is
often antagonism between teachers and journalists. It is a   95
pity because we can be of great help to each other. We share
the desire to broaden the horizons of our young people—and
their parents. We share the desire to enrich the community
in which we find ourselves. We share the desire to foster
constructive criticism in the search for a better way of life.   100

(a) In about 60 words restate the points which this article makes in defence of newspapers as a whole
(b) In about 90 words explain this writer's ideas of the function of a provincial newspaper
(c) Choose an appropriate paragraph, then show how its first sentence states an argument and its later sentences attempt to prove it
(d) Explain in about 60 words why this author thinks newspapers should be studied in school
(e) Write a paragraph in which you refer to newspapers that you yourself read in order to prove, disprove, or illustrate any one argument that this writer puts forward about newspapers

Objective Questions

1   Avid (l. 1) means

    A greedy
    B active
    C insatiable
    D keen
    E enthusiastic

2   The first paragraph stresses, most of all, the fact that newspapers

    A have many faults
    B are widely read in England
    C are finding more readers all over the world
    D are biased and sensational
    E are larger in England than in backward countries

3   'The mud clings to all' (l. 11) means that all newspapers are

    A distrusted
    B sensational
    C too fond of scandal
    D thought badly of
    E criticised

4   'Strictures' (l. 10) are

    A harsh criticisms

B serious faults
C sensational features
D poor reputations
E economic restrictions

5 The second paragraph stresses, most of all, that
   A many criticisms of newspapers are unfair
   B the differences between different newspapers are
      important
   C only a few newspapers deserve to be criticised
   D the quality press is more responsible than the
      popular press
   E more of us ought to read responsible newspapers

6 'Nebulous' (l. 13) means
   A all-embracing
   B comprehensive
   C vague
   D unfair
   E prejudiced

7 The third paragraph argues that school children ought
   to read more than one newspaper; its principal argument
   for this is that it would help them to
   A read more widely
   B obtain useful general information
   C judge between good and bad writing
   D analyse writers' techniques
   E detect various newspapers' political bias

8 'Ersatz emotion' (l. 36) is not
   A healthy
   B strong
   C genuine
   D sentimental
   E unselfish

9   The objectivity of a newspaper means its

   A   passionate resolve to tell the truth
   B   independence from outside influences
   C   freedom from bias
   D   resolve not to be too patriotic
   E   ability to take a wide view

10   'Most school children have much easier access to
   newspapers' (l. 29) means that it is comparatively
   easy for children to

   A   find a newspaper to read
   B   understand a newspaper
   C   take an interest in a newspaper
   D   think it natural to read a newspaper
   E   realise that newspapers have special news sections

11   In saying that newspapers can be used as a stepping-
   stone to literacy, this article does not make clear what is
   meant by 'literacy'. But it must mean the ability to
   read

   A   literature as distinct from journalism
   B   easy reading material, suitable for children
   C   literature written for adults
   D   harder and more worthwhile reading material
   E   a wide range of books and newspapers

12   Lord Williams in *Dangerous Estate* (l. 42) argues that
   the sensational and discreditable news in newspapers

   A   is a correct report of what society is really like
   B   fascinates too many readers
   C   leads some people to stop buying certain news-
       papers
   D   leads millions to buy certain newspapers
   E   proves that Richard Hoggart is right

13   Richard Hoggart (l. 53) argues that the sensational or
   discreditable news in newspapers

   A   is a correct report of what society is really like
   B   omits or distorts the most important news
   C   contains dangerous untruths

D reflects public taste as it is bound to be
E satisfies readers' natural appetites for news

14 The article believes that Richard Hoggart's views are
    A true
    B a simplification of the situation
    C untrue of some newspapers
    D less true than Lord Williams' views
    E important in a democracy

15 This article argues (ll. 65–93) that a local newspaper's
    most important function is to
    A try to remove faults in local society
    B present the truth about local affairs
    C be unbiased
    D praise the community it serves
    E seek to change the course of world affairs

16 'Canalizing their aspirations' (ll. 69–70) means
    A directing their crusading enthusiasms to local
      causes
    B adding a note of realism to their ambitions
    C persuading them to keep to the strict and narrow
      way of moral behaviour
    D giving them more definite ideas of what they
      hope to achieve
    E arousing and encouraging their good resolutions

17 'A newspaper should reflect the community it serves,
    warts and all' (ll. 71-2) means that a local newspaper
    should
    A reveal unpalatable truths
    B interest itself in inter-personal relationships
    C give proper emphasis to local affairs
    D underline the human interest behind the stories
    E not pry too deeply into people's private affairs

18 'The mirror should not be clouded but polished'
(l. 74) means that newspapers should

  A not concern themselves with social justice
  B reveal the worst news most clearly
  C adopt a more moral attitude
  D be forgiven for being sensational
  E be encouraged to reveal defects in society

19 'Eradicated' (l. 75) means

  A clarified
  B discussed
  C improved
  D completely removed
  E investigated

20 'Pretentious' (l. 76) means

  A foolish
  B optimistic
  C snobbish
  D claiming too much
  E hypocritical

21 'The parish-pump mentality' (l. 81) means

  A a one-sided, biased approach to politics
  B an excessive concern for purely local affairs
  C an undue deference to local bigwigs
  D a slavish adherence to tradition
  E a pessimistic tendency to pour cold water over everything

22 One can deduce that this article is taken from a

  A local newspaper
  B newspaper article on the function of the press
  C journal dealing with education
  D book review in a Sunday paper
  E encyclopedia

LIST OF EXTRACTS AND ACKNOWLEDGEMENTS

The following list gives the sources of the extracts included in the book. The authors and publishers make grateful acknowledgement to the authors or authors' executors who have kindly allowed the use of copyright material, and also to the authors' agents and publishers who are mentioned below.

Test 1 Dr Donald Gould: *Cold Comfort*   New Scientist
          Richard Church: *Over the Bridge*   William Heinemann
Test 2 John Hillaby: *Journey Through Britain*

                                              Constable

Test 3 Thor Heyerdahl: *The Kontiki Expedition*

                                    George Allen & Unwin
          Saki: *The Open Window*   The Bodley Head
Test 4 John Stroud: *The Shorn Lamb*   Longman Group
          Garnett Mattingly: *The Defeat of the Spanish Armada*
                                              Jonathan Cape and the
                                              Executors of the
                                              Garnett Mattingly Estate
          J. A. Froude: *English Seamen in the Sixteenth Century*
                                              George Harrap
Test 5 St. Austell Guide   A. L. Rowse
          John Betjeman: *Shell Guide to Cornwall*
                                              Faber and Faber
Test 6 Lieutenant-General Sir William Butler:
              The Life of General Gordon   Macmillan
          Lytton Strachey: *Eminent Victorians*
                      Mrs A. S. Strachey and Chatto & Windus
          Eva Kendall: *Are They Pulling up Old England by
          the Roots?*   Transworld Feature Syndicate
Test 7 Gerald Durrell: *The Overloaded Ark* Faber and Faber
          Dr Franklyn Perring: *Selborne Revisited*
                                              New Scientist
Test 8 Gerald Durrell: *My Family and Other Animals*
                                              Rupert Hart-Davis
          L. T. C. Rolt: *The Inland Waterways of England*
                                    George Allen & Unwin

Test 9 Peter Wilby: *The Lure of Lost Treasure*   The Observer
          Sir Winston Churchill:
             History of the English Speaking Peoples   Cassell
Test 10 A. A. Houghton, N. A. Lund and A. M. Taylor:
             The Food We Live On   Mills and Boon
          Aldous Huxley: *Do What You Will*
                        Mrs Laura Huxley and Chatto & Windus
Test 11 *Derelict Land*   The Civic Trust
          Alan Bullock: *Hitler: A Study in Tyranny*
                           The Hamlyn Publishing Group
Test 12 Jean Anouilh: *Antigone* (translated by Lewis Galantiere)
                              Dr Jan Van Loewen
          Alan Ross: *Australia'55*   Ward Lock Educational
Test 13 Jenny Maitland-Jones: *Careers for Women* The Times
          John Wyndham: *The Day of the Triffids*
                                     Michael Joseph
Test 14 Arnold Hadwin: *The Teacher and the Journalist*
                        Times Educational Supplement

Acknowledgement is also made to the The Solomon R.
Guggenheim Museum, New York, for 'Green Violinist' by
Chagall facing page 96; to Jonathan Cape Ltd. for 'The Mill
Fire' from *And Miss Carter Wore Pink* by Helen Bradley facing
page 128; and to *The Guardian* for the pictures facing pages 97
and 129.